Gamer
Theory

Gamer
Theory

MᶜKENZIE WARK

HARVARD UNIVERSITY PRESS

Cambridge, Massachusetts, and London, England

2007

Many of the designations used by manufacturers and sellers to
distinguish their products are claimed as trademarks. Where
those designations appear in this book and Harvard University
Press was aware of a trademark claim, the designations have
been presented with the capitalization that appears on the man-
ufacturer's official website (PlayStation, *Dungeons & Dragons*,
*SimEarth*, PowerPoint, etc.).

Cataloging-in-Publication Data available from the
Library of Congress

Library of Congress catalog card number: 2006102852
ISBN-13: 978-0-674-02519-6 (alk. paper)
ISBN-10: 0-674-02519-9 (alk. paper)

For Felix
(and his playmates)
*Lude Feliciter*

# Acknowledgments

First, I must thank all of the participants in GAM3R 7H30RY, a "networked book" which presented version 1.1 of this text as a pretext for comments and discussion. For version 2.0, I made many changes to the text on the basis of the comments offered there by gamers, theoryheads, media hackers, and other "organic intellectuals" of the digital age. An edited selection of the comments pertaining directly to the text are included among the notes (Cuts) at the end.

I would also like to thank The Institute for the Future of the Book for hosting GAM3R 7H30RY version 1.1 and for many stimulating discussions. It would not have been half as much fun without Bob Stein, Ben Vershbow, Ray Cha, Dan Visel, and Jesse Wilbur.

I am grateful to my students at Eugene Lang College. Computer games are a key part of the shared culture from which one can begin the process—as laborious as it is playful—of creating a reflective and critical approach to the times. My students at Lang have been active participants in the shaping of the ideas in this book.

Finally, thanks to the terrific team at Harvard University Press, including Lindsay Waters, Phoebe Kosman, Susan Wallace Boehmer, Tim Jones, and Andrew Battle, for the skill and care with which this book has been brought into the world.

Any remaining acts of folly are to be charged directly to my own account.

# CONTENTS

"The unreality of games gives notice that reality is not yet real. Unconsciously they rehearse the right life."

THEODOR ADORNO

"There is an absolute in the moment of the game; and this absolute, like every reality or moment taken to the absolute, represents a specific form of alienation."

HENRI LEFEBVRE

# AGONY

(on *The Cave*)

**E**VER GET THE FEELING you're playing some vast and useless game whose goal you don't know and whose rules you can't remember? Ever get the fierce desire to quit, to resign, to forfeit, only to discover there's no umpire, no referee, no regulator to whom you can announce your capitulation? Ever get the vague dread that while you have no choice but to play the game, you can't win it, can't know the score, or who keeps it? Ever suspect that you don't even know who your real opponent might be? Ever get mad over the obvious fact that the dice are loaded, the deck stacked, the table rigged and the fix—in? Welcome to gamespace. It's everywhere, this atopian arena, this speculation sport. *No pain no gain. No guts no glory. Give it your best shot. There's no second place. Winner take all.* Here's a heads up: In gamespace, even if you *know the deal*, are a *player*, have *got game*, you will notice, all the same, that the game has got you. Welcome to the thunderdome. Welcome to the terrordome. Welcome to *the greatest game of all.* Welcome to *the playoffs, the big league, the masters, the only game in town.* You are a gamer whether you like it or not, now that we all live in a gamespace that is everywhere and nowhere. As Microsoft says: *Where do you want to go today?* You can go anywhere you want in gamespace but you can never leave it.

[002]   SUPPOSE there is a business in your neighborhood called The Cave™. It offers, for an hourly fee, access to game consoles in a darkened room. Suppose it is part of a chain. The consoles form a local area network, and also link to other such networks elsewhere in the chain. Suppose you are a gamer in The Cave. You test your skills against other gamers. You have played in The Cave since childhood.* Your eyes see only the monitor before you. Your ears hear only through the headphones that encase them. Your hands clutch only the controller with which you blast away at the digital figures who shoot back at you on the screen. Here gamers see the images and hear the sounds and say to each other: "Why, these images are just shadows! These sounds are just echoes! The real world is out there somewhere." The existence of another, more real world of which The Cave provides mere copies is assumed, but nobody thinks much of it. Here reigns the wisdom of PlayStation: *Live in your world, play in ours.*

[003]   PERHAPS you are not just any gamer. Perhaps you want to break with the stereotype.* You are the one who decides

to investigate the assumption of a real world beyond the game. You turn away from the screen and unplug the headphones. You get up and stagger out of the darkened room, toward the light outside. You are so dazzled by the light that the people and things out there in the bright world seem less real than the images and sounds of The Cave. You turn away from this blinding new world, which seems, strangely, unreal. You return to the screen and the headphones and the darkness of being a gamer in The Cave.

SUPPOSE someone, a parent maybe, a teacher or some [004] other guardian, drags you back out into the light and makes you stay there. It would still be blinding.* You could not look directly at things. Maybe the guardian prints out some pics of your family or maybe a map of the neighborhood, to acclimatize you, before you can look at things. Gradually you see the people around you and what it is that they do. Then perhaps you remember the immense, immersive games of The Cave, and what passes for wisdom amongst those still stuck there. And so you return to The Cave, to talk or text to the other gamers about this world outside.

YOU COMMUNICATE to fellow gamers in The Cave about the [005] outside world of which The Cave is just a shadow. Or try to. Plato: "And if the cave-dwellers had established, down there in the cave, certain prizes and distinctions for those who were most keen-sighted in seeing the passing shadows, and who were best able to remember what came before, and after, and simultaneously with what, thus best able to predict future appearances in the shadow-world, will our released prisoner hanker after these prizes or envy this power or honor?"* You bet! The Cave is a world of pure agon, of competitive striving after distinction. But suppose you are that rare, stray, thoughtful gamer who decides to try this new game of getting beyond the game one more time? Suppose you emerge from The Cave and decide to take stock of the world beyond? You find that this other world is in some curious ways rather like The Cave. The pics of family, the map of the 'hood, seem made of the same digital stuff as your favorite games inside The Cave. If there is a difference, it may not be quite what it seems.

[006]   HERE IS what you observe about the world outside The Cave: The whole of life appears as a vast accumulation of commodities and spectacles, of things wrapped in images and images sold as things.* But how are these images and things organized, and what role do they call for anyone and everyone to adopt toward them? Images appeal as prizes, and call us to play the game in which they are all that is at stake. You observe that world after world, cave after cave, what prevails is the same agon, the same digital logic of one versus the other, ending in victory or defeat. Agony rules! Everything has value only when ranked against something else; everyone has value only when ranked against someone else. Every situation is win-lose, unless it is win-win—a situation where players are free to collaborate only because they seek prizes in different games. The real world appears as a video arcadia divided into many and varied games. Work is a rat race. Politics is a horse

race. The economy is a casino. Even the utopian justice to come in the afterlife is foreclosed: *He who dies with the most toys wins.* Games are no longer a pastime, outside or alongside of life. They are now the very form of life, and death, and time itself. These games are no joke. When the screen flashes the legend *Game over,* you are either dead, or defeated, or at best out of quarters.

THE GAME has colonized its rivals within the cultural realm, [007] from the spectacle of cinema to the simulations of television. Stories no longer opiate us with imaginary reconciliations of real problems. The story just recounts the steps by which someone beat someone else—a real victory for imaginary stakes. The only original screen genre of the early twenty-first century is not called "reality TV" for nothing. Brenton and Cohen: "By signing their release forms, contestants agree to end up as statistics, each player's feelings and actions manipulated . . . leading to infidelity, tears, perhaps heartbreak." Sure, reality TV doesn't look like reality, but then neither does reality. Both look like games. Both become a seamless space in which gamers test their abilities within contrived scenarios. The situations may be artificial, the dialogue less than spontaneous, and the gamers may merely be doing what the producers tell them. All this is perfectly of a piece with a reality, which is itself an artificial arena, where everyone is born a gamer, waiting for their turn.*

THE GAME has not just colonized reality, it is also the sole [008] remaining ideal.* Gamespace proclaims its legitimacy through victory over all rivals. The reigning ideology imagines the world as a *level playing field*, upon which all folks are equal before God, the great game designer. History, politics, culture—gamespace dynamites everything that is not in the game, like an outdated Vegas casino. Everything is evacuated from an empty space and time which now appears natural, neutral, and without qualities—a gamespace. The lines are clearly marked. Every action is just a means to an end. All that counts is the score. As for who owns the teams and who runs the show, best not to ask. As for who is excluded from the big leagues, best not to ask. As for who keeps the score and who makes the rules, best not to ask. As for what ruling body does the handicapping and on what basis, best not to ask. All is for the best in the best—and only—possible world. There is—to give it a name—a military entertainment complex, and it *rules*. Its triumphs affirm not just the rules of the game but the rule of the game.

[009] **EVERYTHING** the military entertainment complex touches with its gold-plated output jacks turns to digits. Everything is digital and yet the digital is as nothing. No human can touch it, smell it, taste it. It just beeps and blinks and reports itself in glowing alphanumerics, spouting stock quotes on your cell phone. Sure, there may be vivid 3D graphics. There may be pie charts and bar graphs. There may be swirls and whorls of brightly colored polygons blazing from screen to screen. But these are just decoration. The jitter of your thumb on the button or the flicker of your wrist on the mouse connect directly to an invisible, intangible gamespace of pure contest, pure agon. It doesn't

matter if your cave comes equipped with a PlayStation or Bloomberg terminal. It doesn't matter whether you think you are playing the bond market or *Grand Theft Auto*. It is all just an algorithm with enough unknowns to make a game of it.

ONCE GAMES required an actual place to play them, whether on the chess board or the tennis court. Even wars had battle *fields*. Now global positioning satellites grid the whole earth and put all of space and time in play. Warfare, they say, now looks like video games. Well don't kid yourself. War *is* a video game—for the military entertainment complex. To them it doesn't matter what happens *on the ground*. The ground—the old-fashioned battlefield itself— is just a necessary externality to the game. Slavoj Žižek: "It is thus not the fantasy of a purely aseptic war run as a video game behind computer screens that protects us from the reality of the face to face killing of another person; on the contrary it is this fantasy of face to face encounter with an enemy killed bloodily that we construct in order to escape the Real of the depersonalized war turned into an anonymous technological operation."* Even the soldier whose inadequate armor failed him, shot dead in an alley by a sniper, has his death, like his life, managed by a computer in a blip of logistics.

THE OLD class antagonisms have not gone away but are hidden beneath levels of rank, where each agonizes over their worth against others as measured by the size of their house and the price of their vehicle and where, perversely,

[010]

[011]

working longer and longer hours is a sign of victory. Work becomes play. Work demands not just one's mind and body but also one's soul. You have to be a *team player*. Your work has to be creative, inventive, playful—ludic, but not ludicrous. Work becomes a gamespace, but no games are freely chosen any more. Not least for children, who if they are to be the winsome offspring of win-all parents, find themselves drafted into endless evening shifts of team sport. The purpose of which is to *build character*. Which character? The character of the *good sport*. Character for what? For the workplace, with its team camaraderie and peer-enforced discipline. For others, work is still just dull, repetitive work, but they dream of escaping into the commerce of play—making it into the major leagues, or competing for record deals as a *diva* or a *playa* in the *rap game*. And for still others, there is only the game of survival. Biggie: "Either you're slingin' crack rock or you got a wicked jump shot."* Play becomes everything to which it was once opposed. It is work, it is serious; it is morality, it is necessity.

[012]  **THE OLD** identities fade away. Nobody has the time. The gamer is not interested in playing the citizen.* The law is fine as a spectator sport on *Court TV,* but being a citizen just involves endless attempts to get out of jury duty. Got a problem? Tell it to *Judge Judy*. The gamer elects to choose sides only for the purpose of the game. This week it might be as the Alliance vs. the Horde. Next week it might be as the Earth vs. the Covenant. If the gamer chooses to be a soldier and play with real weapons, it is as an *Army of One,*

testing and refining personal skill points. The shrill and constant patriotic noise you hear through the speakers masks the slow erosion of any coherent fellow feeling within the remnants of national borders. This gamespace escapes all checkpoints. It is an America without qualities, for everybody and nobody. All that is left of the nation is an everywhere that is nowhere, an atopia of noisy, righteous victories and quiet, sinister failures. Manifest destiny—the right to rule through virtue—gives way to its latent destiny—the virtue of right through rule. Civic spirit drowns in a hurricane of mere survivalism.

THE GAMER is not really interested in faith, although a [013] heightened rhetoric of faith may fill the void carved out of the soul by the insinuations of gamespace. The gamer's God is a game designer. He implants in everything a hidden algorithm. Faith is having the intelligence to intuit the parameters of this geek design and score accordingly. All that is righteous wins; all that wins is righteous. To be a *loser* or a *lamer* is the mark of damnation. When you are a gamer, you are left with nothing to believe in but your own God-given abilities. Gamers confront one another in contests of skill that reveal who has been *chosen*—chosen by the game as the one who has most fully internalized its algorithm. For those who despair of their abilities, there are games of chance, where grace reveals itself in the roll of the dice. Roger Caillois: "Chance is courted because hard work and personal qualifications are powerless to bring such success about."* The gambler may know what the gamer's faith refuses to countenance.

[014] OUTSIDE each cave is another cave; beyond the game is another game. Each has its particular rules; each has its ranks of high scores. Is that all there is? The gamer who lifts an eye from the target risks a paralyzing boredom. Paolo Virno: "At the base of contemporary cynicism is the fact that men and women learn by experiencing rules rather than 'facts' . . . Learning the rules, however, also means recognizing their unfoundedness and conventionality . . . We now face several different 'games,' each devoid of all obviousness and seriousness, only the site of an immediate self-affirmation—an affirmation that is much more brutal and arrogant, much more cynical, the more we employ, with no illusions but with perfect momentary adherence, those very rules whose conventionality and mutability we have perceived."* Each game ends in a summary decision: *That's Hot!* Or if not, *You're Fired!* Got questions about qualities of Being? *Whatever.*

[015] SO THIS is the world as it appears to the gamer: a matrix of endlessly varying games—a gamespace—all reducible to the same principles, all producing the same kind of subject who belongs to this gamespace in the same way, as a gamer to a game. What would it mean to lift one's eye from the target, to pause on the trigger, to unclench one's ever-clicking finger? Is it even possible to think outside The Cave? Perhaps with the triumph of gamespace, what the gamer as theorist needs is to reconstruct the deleted files on those who thought pure play could be a radical option, who opposed gamespace with their revolutionary playdates. The Situationists, for example. Raoul Vaneigem:

"Subversion . . . is an all embracing reinsertion of things into play. It is the act whereby play grasps and reunites beings and things hitherto frozen solid in a hierarchy of fragments." Play, yes, but the game—no. Guy Debord: "I have scarcely begun to make you understand that I don't intend to play the game." Now *there* was a player unconcerned with an exit strategy.*

"PLAY" WAS once a great slogan of liberation. Richard [016] Neville: "The new beautiful freaks will teach us all how to play again (and they'll suffer society's penalty)."* Play was once the battering ram to break down the Chinese walls of alienated work, of divided labor. Only look at what has become of play. Play is no longer a counter to work. Play becomes work; work becomes play. Play outside of work found itself captured by the rise of the digital game, which responds to the boredom of the player with endless rounds of repetition, level after level of difference as more of the same. Play no longer functions as a foil for a critical theory. The utopian dream of liberating play from the game, of a pure play beyond the game, merely opened the way for the extension of gamespace into every aspect of everyday life. While the counter-culture wanted worlds of play outside the game, the military entertainment complex countered in turn by expanding the game to the whole world, containing play forever within it.

EVEN CRITICAL theory, which once took its distance from [017] damaged life, becomes another game. Apply to top-ranked schools. Find a good coach. Pick a rising subfield. Prove your abilities. Get yourself published. Get some grants. Get a job. Get another job offer to establish your level in bargaining with your boss. Keep your nose clean and get tenure. You won! Now you can play! Now you can do what you secretly wanted to do all those years ago . . . Only now you can't remember. You became a win-win Situationist. Your critical theory became hypocritical theory. It is against everything in the whole wide world except the gamespace that made itself possible. But gamespace is now the very form of the world, and this world eluded your thought even as it brought home the glittering prizes. It is gamespace that won. The hypocritical theorist, in an agony of fitful sleep, dreams of meeting the ghost of Guy Debord and proudly citing a list of achievements: Ivy League job, book deals, grants, promotion, tenure, recognition within the highest ranks of the disciplinary guild. The ghost of Debord sighs: "So little ambition in one so young."

[018] WHAT THEN has the gamer seen in that bright world, that gamespace, beyond The Cave? You see people hunched over screens, their hands compulsively jerking controllers. Each sits alone, and talks or texts to unseen others, dazzled by images that seem to come from nowhere, awash in pulsing and beeping sounds. No one out here in the "real world" really looks all that different to the stereotypical gamer, thumb mashing the controller. Now you are an enlightened gamer, you see how the world beyond the games of The Cave seems like an array of more or less similar caves, all digital, each an agon with its own rules, some ar-

bitrary blend of chance and competition. And beyond that? Not much. The real has become mere detritus without which gamespace cannot exist but which is losing, bit by bit, any form or substance or spirit or history that is not sucked into and transformed by gamespace. Beyond gamespace appear only the spent fragments of nameless forms.

GAMER THEORY starts with a suspension of the assumptions of The Cave: that there is a more real world beyond it, somewhere, and that someone—some priest or professor—knows where it is. The gamer arrives at the beginnings of a reflective life, a gamer theory, by stepping out of The Cave—and returning to it (see Fig. A). If the gamer is to hold gamespace to account in terms of something other than itself, it might not be that mere shadow of a shadow of the real, murky, formless that lurks like a residue in the corners. It might instead be the game proper, as it is played in The Cave. *Grand Theft Auto*, maybe, or *Deus Ex*. Here at least the game shadows the ideal form of the algorithm. Here at least the digital logic to which gamespace merely aspires is actually realized. The challenge is—ah, but even to phrase it thus is to acknowledge the game—to play at play itself, but from within the game. The gamer as theorist has to choose between two strategies for playing against gamespace. One is to play for the real (Take the red pill). But the real seems nothing but a heap of broken images. The other is to play for the game (Take the blue pill). Play within the game, but against gamespace. Be ludic, but also lucid.

[019]

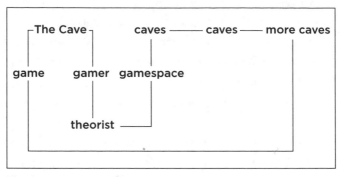

Fig. A

[020] FOR A gamer to be a theorist might not require the ability to play any particular game especially well. The prizes have nothing to do with thinking the game. Nor might gamer theory be the ability to dismiss the game as unreal in the name of some supposedly more solidly grounded outside. What? These luminous pixels are not real, you say? Then neither is *your* world. If anything, The Cave seems to be where the forms, the ideas, the abstractions behind the mere appearance of things in the outside world can be found. Whether gamespace is more real or not than some other world is not the question; that even in its unreality it may have real effects on other worlds *is*. Games are not representations of this world. They are more like allegories of a world made over as gamespace. They encode the abstract principles upon which decisions about the realness of this or that world are now decided.

[021] HERE IS the guiding principle of a future utopia, now long past: "To each according to his needs; from each according

to his abilities."* In gamespace, what do we have? An atopia, a placeless, senseless realm where quite a different maxim rules: "From each according to their abilities—to each a rank and score." Needs no longer enter into it. Not even desire matters. Uncritical gamers do not win what they desire; they desire what they win. The score is the thing. The rest is agony. The gamer as theorist at first sight seems to have acquired an ability that counts for nothing in gamespace. The gamer as theorist might begin with an indifference to distinction, to all that the gamespace prizes. You do not play the game to win (or not just to win). You trifle with it—playing with style to understand the game as a form. You trifle with the game to understand the nature of gamespace as a world—as *the* world. You trifle with the game to discover in what way gamespace falls short of its self-proclaimed perfection. The digital game plays up everything that gamespace merely pretends to be: *a fair fight, a level playing field, unfettered competition.*

NO WONDER digital games are the emergent cultural form [022] of our time. The times have themselves become just a series of less and less perfect games. The Cave presents games in a pure state, as a realm where justice—of a sort—reigns. The beginnings of a critical theory of games—a gamer theory—might lie not in holding games accountable as failed representations of the world, but quite the reverse. The world outside is a gamespace that appears as an imperfect form of the computer game. The gamer is an archeologist of The Cave. The computer games that the gamer finds there are the ruins not of a lost past but of an impossible future. Gamespace is built on the ruins of a future it proclaims in theory yet disavows in practice. The gamer theorist is not out to break the game. To the extent that the gamer theorist wants to hack or "mod" the game, it is to play even more intimately within it.* The point is not to reduce the game to the level of the imperfect world outside it. Like any archeologist, the gamer theorist treats these ruins of the future with obsessive care and attention to their preservation, not their destruction.

[023] GAMESPACE needs theorists—but also a new kind of practice. One that can break down the line that divides gamer from designer, to redeploy the digital so that it makes this very distinction arbitrary. It is a characteristic of games to render digital decisions on all shades of difference. One either wins or loses. One either hits or misses. The practice of the gamer as theorist might be to reinstall what is undecidable back into the gamespace whose primary violence has nothing to do with brightly colored explosions or mounting death counts but with the decision by digital fiat on where everything belongs and how it is ranked. Lars Svendsen: "How boring life would be without violence!" The real violence of gamespace is its dicing of everything analog into the digital, cutting continuums into bits. That games present the digital in its most pure form are reason enough to embrace them, for here violence is at its most extreme—and its most harmless.*

[024] OF ALL the kinds of belonging that contend for allegiance—as workers against the boss, as citizens against

the enemy, as believers against the infidel—all now have to compete with one which makes agon its first and only principle. Gamespace wants us to believe we are all nothing but gamers now, competing not against enemies of class or faith or nation but only against other gamers. A new historical persona slouches toward the ergonomic chair to be born. All of the previous such persona had many breviaries and manuals, and so this little book in your hands seeks to offer guidance for thinking within this new persona. An ABC of theory for gamers. Not a strategy guide, a cheat sheet, or a walk-through for how to improve your score or hone your trigger finger. A primer, rather, in thinking about a world made over as a gamespace, made over as an imperfect copy of the game. The game might not be utopia, but it might be the only thing left with which to play against gamespace.

**NO WONDER** gamers choose to spend their time holed up [025] in The Cave. Here at least the targets really are only polygons and the prizes really are worthless, mere colors and numbers. These are not the least of its merits. And yet The Cave is a world you can neither own nor control. Even this dub for utopia is in someone else's possession. The digital game is both an almost utopian alternative to gamespace and its most pure product. Or was. Perhaps the game is collapsing back into business as usual. Perhaps the single-player game will become an anachronism, superseded by multiplayer worlds as venal and benighted as the rest of gamespace.* Perhaps, like silent cinema, the stand-alone game will be an orphaned form. Perhaps game designers such as Will Wright and Tetsuya Mizugushi will be the Sergei Eisensteins and Dziga Vertovs of a lost art. Perhaps, in this moment of eclipse, the classic games have something to show us. So by all means necessary, be a gamer, but be a gamer who thinks—and acts—with a view to realizing the real potentials of the game, in and against this world made over as a gamespace. You might start with the curious gap between the games you love and an everyday life which, by the light of the game, seems curiously similar, and yet somehow lacking.

# ALLEGORY
## (on *The Sims*)

**B**ENJAMIN GETS UP in the morning. He 〔026〕 goes to the toilet. He leaves the seat up. He showers and fixes breakfast. He reads the paper. He finds a job—as a Test Subject—starting tomorrow. It's not much, but times are hard. He reads a book, and then another. He fixes lunch, naps, reads again. He goes to bed. He gets up. Toilet, shower, breakfast again. He does not make his bed. He goes to work. He comes home, prepares another meal. He talks to his roommate Bert a bit. Hannah drops by. He flirts with her some. He goes to bed, gets up, does the whole thing all over again.

DAYS go by. Not much changes. His cooking improves. He 〔027〕 makes new friends—Ted, Gersholm, Asja. They drop by sometimes; sometimes he visits them. There is new furniture. That makes him a bit happier, but not much. He gets a promotion to Lab Assistant. It's the night shift, but the pay is better. Then he makes Field Researcher and is back working regular hours. After some effort he becomes a Scholar. He is so creative, but it helps to have friends if you want to get ahead. He aspires to being a Theorist. The pay is better. And the hours. He dreams of yachts and big screen TVs. Benjamin is a Sim, a character in a game called *The Sims*. One could be forgiven for imagining this was somebody's life.

[028]   IN *THE SIMS*, you create characters like Benjamin, build and furnish homes for them, find them jobs and friends. All in a world without a sky. Perhaps a game like *The Sims* could be a parody of everyday life in "the society of the spectacle." Benjamin and his friends dream of things. Things make them happy. They find a nice sofa so much more relaxing than a cheap one. As the game's designer Will Wright says: "If you sit there and build a big mansion that's all full of stuff, without cheating, you realize that all these objects end up sucking up all your time, when all these objects had been promising to save you time . . . And it's actually kind of a parody of consumerism, in which at some point your stuff takes over your life." Others disagree. Game scholar Gonzalo Frasca: "Certainly, the game may be making fun of suburban Americans, but since it rewards the player every time she buys new stuff, I do not think this could be considered parody." In *The Sims*, characters can have lots of different jobs, but as Fredric Jameson says: "Parody finds itself without a vocation."*

PERHAPS a game like *The Sims* could be an allegory for everyday life in gamespace. In the allegorical mode, says Walter Benjamin: "Any person, any object, any relationship can mean absolutely anything else. With this possibility a destructive but just verdict can be passed on the profane world: it is characterized as a world in which the detail is of no great importance." For Benjamin, the fragmenting of the modern world by technique, the profusion of commodities that well up in the absence of a coherent whole, finds its expression in allegory, which fragments things still further, shattering the illusion of bourgeois order, revealing the means by which it is made. "What resists the mendacious transfiguration of the commodity world is its distortion into allegory." And yet this possibility too seems exhausted. The fragmenting of the fragmented seems routine to a Sim. No other world seems possible.* 〖029〗

PERHAPS a game like *The Sims* is not just an allegory but also an "allegorithm." Being a gamer is a different persona to being a reader or a viewer. Lev Manovich: "As the player proceeds through the game, she gradually discovers the rules that operate in the universe constructed by this game." Alex Galloway: "To play the game means to play the code of the game. To win means to know the system. And thus to interpret a game means to interpret its algorithm (to discover its parallel allegorithm)." What is distinctive about games is that they produce for the gamer an intuitive relation to the algorithm. The intuitive experience and the organizing algorithm together are an allegorithm for a 〖030〗

future that in gamespace is forever promised but never comes to pass. The allegorithm by which the gamer relates to the algorithm produces a quite particular allegory by which gamer and algorithm together relate to gamespace. In a game, any character, any object, any relationship can be given a value, and that value can be discovered. With this possibility, a challenging but fair verdict can be passed on the profane world: it is characterized as a world in which any value is arbitrary, yet its value and its relation to other values can be discovered through trial and error.*

[031] AN ALGORITHM—for present purposes—is a finite set of instructions for accomplishing some task, which transforms an initial starting condition into a recognizable end condition. The recipes that Benjamin and other Sims learn from the cookbooks on their bookshelves are algorithms. Benjamin's career as a Theorist is also an algorithm. There is a start condition: he must have 8 friends, 4 charisma points, a 7 in creativity, and so on. It has end conditions, too. With 10 friends, 5 charisma points, and 10 for creativity, the Theorist career can end and another begin. Greg Costikyan: "Algorithmic games are ones in which underlying calculations or rules determine the game's response to the player's input."* The gamer selects one sequence after another, and gradually learns what they do—that's algorithm. The gamer discovers a relationship between appearances and algorithm in the game, which is a double of the relation between appearances and a putative algorithm in gamespace—that's allegorithm (see Fig. B). But there is always a gap between the intuitively knowable algorithm of

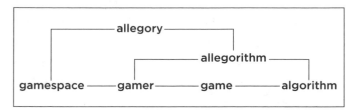

**Fig. B**

the game and the passing, uneven, unfair semblance of an algorithm in the everyday life of gamespace—this is the form that allegory now takes.

THE IMAGES and stories that populate games are mostly [032] cribbed from other media—from novels, films, or television. Games mostly just recycle, or "remediate," bits of representation from other media. Bolter and Grusin: "Remediation is a defining characteristic of the new digital media."* And hence not specific to games. What is specific to games is at the level of form, not content. From the point of view of representation, the game is always inadequate to everyday life. A Sim in *The Sims* is a simple animated character, with few facial features or expressions. In *The Sims 2* they seem a little more lifelike, but the improvement of the representation in some particular ways only raises the standards by which it appears to fall short in others. From the point of view of allegorithm, it all seems more the other way around. Everyday life in gamespace seems an imperfect version of the game. The gamespace of everyday life may be more complex and variegated, but it seems much less consistent, coherent, and fair. Perhaps this was always the atopian promise of the digital—a real of absolute, impersonal equity and equanimity. The game opens a critical gap between what gamespace promises and what it delivers. What is true is not real; what is real is not true. This is what the double movement of allegorithm and allegory have to report. The game is true in that its algorithm is consistent, but this very consistency negates a world that is not.

[033]   IMAGINE that Benjamin makes it to the penultimate level and becomes a Theorist. Perhaps then you buy him a computer because he seems bored with reading. What would he do with it? Play *The Sims,* of course. Being a Theorist, perhaps he starts to think about it. Perhaps he jots something like this in his notebook: "The gamer whose listless gaze falls on the controller in his hand is ready for the allegorithm. Boredom is the basis of the allegorithmic insight into the world. Boredom lays waste to the appeal of the game as game, and calls attention to the ambiguous relation of game to gamespace. Allegorithmic perception is n-dimensional, it intuits behind appearances interactions of many variables. The allegorithmic mode of apprehension is always built on an evaluative relation to the world of appearances. More and more relentlessly, the everyday life of gamers is coming to wear the expression of gamespace. At the same time, gamespace seeks to disguise the ungamelike character of things. What heightens the mendacious transformation of gamespace is its appearance in an undistorted form in the game. Still, gamespace wants to look itself in the face. It celebrates its incarnation in the gamer."

IN THE gamer, Benjamin might say, is reborn the sort of idler that Socrates picked out from the Athenian market- place to be his interlocutor. "Only, there is no longer a Soc- rates, so there is no one to address the idler. And the slave labor that guaranteed him his leisure has likewise ceased to exist."* In *The Sims,* as in gamespace, one wonders if the idler has disappeared also. There is no idle time in *The Sims,* or in the gamespace of which it is the more perfect double. The quartz heart of the computer on which *The Sims* runs ticks over remorselessly. All of its moments are equivalent, and so too, in a way, are all moments in *The Sims.* Sleeping, napping, conversation, or reading all ad- vance one's scores. Benjamin has to go to bed to get up again to go to work to earn the right to sleep, and dream, again.

TO BE a gamer is to come to understanding through quantifiable failure. The bar graphs measuring Benjamin's being ebb toward the negative and refuse to budge. You are too busy elsewhere to get Benjamin to the toilet on time, and so he pees on himself. He needs sleep, he needs love, he needs a new kitchen. He turns to face you, the gamer, and gestures wildly, as if cursing his God. When things were going well, you forgot to save the game, so there is no better time to go back to. Nothing for it but to work with what you have, or quit and start again. The game is a knowable algorithm from which you know you can escape; gamespace is an unknown algorithm from which there is no escape. The game is just like the gamespace of everyday life, except that the game can be saved. The game can overcome the violence of time. The game ties up that one loose end with which gamespace struggles—the mortal flaw of an irreversible time. No wonder the Sim turns in vain to the gamer as a God, for it is the gamer who has turned toward the game as a messianic, reversible time.

[036] **GAMERS ARE** not always good Gods. It's such a temptation to set up a Sim to suffer. Deprive them of a knowledge of cooking and pretty soon they set fire to themselves. Build a house without doors or windows and they starve. Watch as the algorithm works itself out to its terminal state, the bar graphs sliding down to nothing. This violence is not "real." Sims are not people. They are images. They are images in a world that appears as a vast accumulation of images. Hence the pleasure in destroying images, to demonstrate again and again their worthlessness. They can mean anything and nothing. They have no saving power. But even though the images are meaningless, the algorithm still functions. It assigns, if not meaning, if not veracity, if not necessity, then at least a score to representations.* In *The Sims* the world of gamespace is redeemed by providing for its myriad things the algorithm that they lack to form consistent relations.

[037] **THE SIM** who suffers turns to face its gamer, looking out toward an absent sky, appealing directly, beyond the frame of the game itself. The gamer may not answer, or may not be able to answer. The gamer as God suffers from an apparently similar algorithmic logic as the Sim. *The Sims* comes with theological options. Turn on "free will" and Sims stray

from the powers of their maker. Turn it off and their actions are predestined, but even so the gamer-God quickly finds that the algorithm is a higher power than the power one commands. Should the game be going badly for the Sim, it turns to face the gamer; should the game be going badly for the gamer, there is no one for the gamer to turn away and face. The Sim who addresses a helpless, hopeless, or lost God lives out the allegory of gamespace itself. At least the Sim has someone to turn to. Who can the gamer turn to? Perhaps you can see now the reason for the popularity, among those troubled by gamespace but lacking a concept to account for it, of a personal God who can perform miracles, who can break the rules of his own algorithm.

AS A gamer you can have no sense of worth and no faith in salvation other than through your own efforts. But those efforts are fraught, and you are soon lost in the maze of the game. The gamer achieves worth through victories of character; but that character inevitably faces defeat in turn. Or worse. The only thing worse than being defeated is being undefeated. For then there is nothing against which to secure the worth of the gamer other than to find another game. One game leads to the next. It's the same for Benjamin. After Theorist comes Mad Scientist and after that—nothing. Start over. Pick a new career. Get an expansion pack. Try some new lives. Start as a Playground Monitor, become a Teacher, a Professor, get tenure, rise to Dean, then finally, Minister of Education. Start as a Nobody, working for tips. Become an Insider, a Name Dropper, a Sell-

Out, a Player, a Celebrity, then finally, a Superstar. But these are just arbitrary names for series of levels. Any qualitative difference between levels is just the effect of an underlying quantity. A higher level is essentially *more* than a lower level. And so there's nowhere to go but to more, and more, until there is no more, and the gamer, like the character, is left with nothing. The fruit of the digital is the expulsion of quality from the world. That's gamespace. The consolation of the game is that at least this expulsion is absolute.

⟦039⟧ ORIGINAL Sims can be any mix of two genders and three colors. In *The Sims 2* you start with preset templates (Caucasian, African American, Chinese, Persian—and Elf) alterable via a lot of sub-sliders. You choose gender, age, color, hair style and color, eye color, weight, height, glasses, hats, accessories, clothes, and so on, but these external attributes are merely a skin. They do not really affect the game. The sliding variables of character, however, do program in advance what careers a Sim can excel at, and which past times restore faculties. In *Sims 2,* they may be straight or gay. Again, it makes no difference. Either way their offspring mix the "genetic" character qualities of their parents. The external representations are of no account; the internal variables determine potential. The "skin" is arbitrary, a difference without a distinction, mere decoration. Underneath it lies a code which is all. *The Sims 2* is committed both to a genetic view of intrinsic nature and a liberal view of the equality, and hence indifference, of extrinsic appearances.

IN *THE SIMS* things proliferate. Or rather the skins of [040] things. You can have many different kinds of sofa, or coffee table, or lamp shade, but the meter is running, so to speak. You have to make more money to buy more things. But some gamers who play *The Sims* trifle with the game rather than play it. These gamers are not interested in "winning" the game, they are interested in style, in details, in furniture, or telling stories, or creating interesting worlds. If a cheat is someone who ignores the space of a game to cut straight to its objective, then the trifler is someone who ignores the objective to linger within its space. Bernard Suits: "Triflers recognize rules but not goals, cheats recognize goals but not rules." *The Sims* lends itself to play that transforms it from a world of number back to a world of meaning. Algorithm becomes a more stable platform than the vicissitudes of gamespace for creating a suburban world of pretty things. But in trifling with the game, the gamer struggles to escape boredom and produce difference—and finds that this too has limits. Steven Poole: "You must learn the sequences the programmers have built in to the game—and, okay, there are hundreds of them, but that does not constitute freedom." Games redeem gamespace by offering a perfect unfreedom, a consistent set of constraints.*

ALLEGORY is about the relation of sign to sign; allegorithm [041] is about the relation of sign to number. Signs don't open to reveal chains of other signs, pointing in all directions. Or rather, it is no longer of any importance what signs reveal. They billow and float, pool and gather, arbitrary and useless. There is no way to redeem them. But signs now point to something else. They point to number. And number in turn points to the algorithm, which transforms one number into another, then stops. Out of the bit rot of signs, games make allegorithms. The signs point to numbers, the numbers to algorithms, the algorithms to allegorithms of everyday life in gamespace, where signs likewise are devalued, arbitrary, but can still stand as allegories of the one thing that still makes sense, for the logic of the digital.

[042]  ALLEGORY becomes a double relation: on the one side, there is the relation of gamer to algorithm in the game, its allegorithm; on the other, there is the relation of allegorithm to everyday life in gamespace. In relation to gamespace, the game itself works as an escape from the agony of everyday life, where the stakes are real and uncertain, to the unreal stakes of a pure game. But the game can also work as a critique, in turn, of the unreality of the stakes of gamespace itself. When *Sims* devotees assign values to nonexistent furniture, truly the idea of economic "utility" has lost all meaning. The game can also work as an "atopia," where play is free from work, from necessity, from seriousness, from morality. Kill your Sims, if you want to. Play here has no law but the algorithm. And yet there is a tension between the game and gamespace. The relation between them is at once analog and digital, both a continuum and a sharp break. The gamer struggles to make of the game a separate world, for escape, for critique, for atopian play, and yet gamespace insinuates itself into the game.

START OVER: Benjamin begins as a Beta Tester, becomes a [043] Hacker, and finally a Game Designer. After that you are supposed to level up to Venture Capitalist then finally Information Overlord. But something goes wrong along the way. Benjamin's game design company goes broke. The whole industry is consolidating. So Benjamin goes to work for a much bigger game company. He starts work. It's a mild sort of *crunch time*—normal when there's a project with a deadline. Benjamin is working eight hours, six days a week. The project is on schedule, so it's not so bad. It's temporary. He complains a bit to Asja. The deadline for ending the crunch comes and goes. And another. Then the hours get longer. Benjamin is working twelve hours, six days a week. Benjamin's bar graphs slide into the red. Then the real crunch time begins. Benjamin is working seven days a week, "with the occasional Saturday evening off for good behavior."*

YOU COULD be forgiven for thinking this is just a game, [044] but it is somebody's life—as reported in a widely circulated text written by EA Spouse. EA, or Electronic Arts, is a game company best known for its *Madden* sports games but which also owns Maxis, which makes *The Sims*. EA's slogan: *Challenge Everything*—everything except EA, of course, or the gap between game and gamespace. In the gamespace of contemporary labor, things are not like the measured progression up the ranks of *The Sims*. In *The Sims,* Benjamin could work his way from Game Designer to Information Overlord much the same way as he had worked up the levels below. At Electronic Arts, things are different. Being an Information Overlord like EA's Larry Probst requires an army of Benjamins with nothing to work with but their skills as game designers and nowhere to go other than to another firm which may or may not crunch its workers just as hard. As the military entertainment complex consolidates into a handful of big firms, it squeezes out all but a few niche players. Gamespace is here a poor imitation of its own game.

[045] START OVER again: This time Benjamin begins as a Bucket Runner. He quickly works himself up to Coltan Miner. Coltan? What is coltan? Quit *The Sims* for a moment. Pop the cover off your PlayStation or your laptop or cell phone. You are looking at stuff that has come from all over the world—brought together by a global logistics. In the guts of your machine you may spot some capacitors made by Kemet, or maybe semiconductors from Intel. These probably contain tantalum, a marvelous conductor of electricity, also very good with heat. They were quite possibly made with coltan (short for columbite-tantalite) dug out of the ground in the Congo, where there's plenty of coltan, from which tantalum is refined. The Okapi Faunal Reserve in the Congo is home to gorillas, monkeys, and elephants as well as the okapi, a rare relative of the giraffe. Thousands of Mbuti, or pygmies, also live there. Their livelihood is compromised by the coltan miners, who dig what one journalist called "SUV-sized holes" in the mud, out of which they can extract about a kilo of coltan a day. A kilo of coltan was worth $80 during the technology boom. There

was a world shortage of the stuff, which even delayed the release of the Sony PlayStation 2.*

THE CONGO is arguably the region in which the "great   [046]
game" of colonial exploitation has done the most harm and conferred the least benefit. The Congo's first democratic leader, Patrice Lumumba, was ousted in a CIA-sponsored coup that brought to power the notorious Mobutu Sese Seku. With the collapse of the Mobutu regime, there was civil war—and uncivil war. One of the things that kept the civil war going was the coltan. Coltan both fueled the war and accelerated the destruction of wildlife habitats. And so the military entertainment complex, with precious brands to protect, didn't want protest movements sullying their reputations by calling attention to all the gorillas coltan kills, or the guerrillas it feeds. The military entertainment complex would like to believe, and would like you to believe, that gamespace is not a Nietzschian struggle of naked forces, beyond good and evil, but a clean, well-lighted, rule-governed game.

"KEMET requires its suppliers to certify that their coltan   [047]
ore does not originate from Congo or bordering countries." Motorola says: "We believe we have done as much as any reasonable company could do by mandating compliance from our suppliers on this important issue." Outi Mikkonen, communications manager for environmental affairs at Nokia, is a little more sanguine: "All you can do is ask, and if they say no, we believe it." The bad publicity

around Congo coltan is good news for the Australian company Sons of Gwalia, which now provides much of the world supply. The destruction of Australian habitats seems somehow less picturesque. No gorillas or giraffes are involved. This is the way it's played in gamespace. It's all separate caves, with dim reports of each other. By all means, save the gorillas and okapi, but it doesn't change the equation.*

[048] **THE LINE** that connects gamespace to game also divides one from the other. There's no getting away from the materials that make it possible to own a PlayStation console or a computer with *Intel Inside*. There's no getting away from the labor that makes it possible to run *The Sims* on your machine. Benjamin: "There is no document of culture which is not at the same time a document of barbarism."* Benjamin (the Sim): "There is no realm of the pure digit which does not betray the hand marked with muck and blood, somewhere." And yet the whole point of a game is its separation, the line dividing it from gamespace and enclosing it in a self-contained algorithmic world of its own. To Benjamin—the Benjamin who is a Sim—everything outside *The Sims* is just metaphysics. The double relation of allegory and allegorithm is an intimate line alternately connecting and separating game from gamespace.

[049] *THE SIMS* is a very peculiar kind of game, in which everyday life is the subject of play but where play is nothing but work. And yet there's a difference between play in a game

and play in gamespace, which permits the former to offer an allegory for the latter, an allegory which may function as escape and critique of gamespace, perhaps even as an atopian alternative. In the game, unlike in gamespace, the contest between gamer and game is over nothing. There are no precious minerals. There is no labor contract in dispute. The difference between play and its other may have collapsed, but there is still a difference between play within the bounds of an algorithm that works impersonally, the same for everybody, and a gamespace that appears as nothing but an agon for the will to power—whether of guerrillas' grasping their gun stocks or Larry Probst grasping his stock options. If it is a choice only between *The Sims* as a real game and gamespace as a game of the real, the gamer chooses to stay in The Cave and play games. The contradiction is that for there to be a game which is fair and rational there must be a gamespace which is neither.

THE GAME is what gamespace isn't, particularly for those [050] for whom it is the dominant cultural form. EA Spouse writes: "We both have been steeped in essentially game culture from an early age, and we watched that 'culture' gain legitimacy as we got to the point of thinking about our future careers." The gamespace of making games as commodities cannot live up to the games themselves. On EA Spouse's website, some forlorn gamer has written, and perhaps again in vain: "On the simes busten out please do not make a meter for the items you buy. Same with walls or aniny thing eles. So bottom line no metter in any of the simes games ever again please. Thank you if you do it." But, sadly, the meter is always running. It is integral to gamespace, if not necessarily to what makes gamespace possible. Beyond the critique of actually existing gamespace, games can point also to an atopian promise, in which games are something else again. But while the game opens toward new worlds, gamespace forecloses anything but its own relentless agon.*

# AMERICA

(on *Civilization III*)

**O**F WHAT USE IS THE PAST to a gamer? Peter Lunenfeld: "For the most part, it's blood, mischief and role playing that gamers revel in. They live in an alternative universe, a solipsistic one scripted by designers whose frame of reference extends no further back than *Pong, Pac-Man,* and *Dungeons & Dragons.* The visual and storyline tropes that most of us bring with us as cultural baggage are . . . all but forgotten ancestral memories, thrown off, on purpose, too cumbersome to be of any use."* In this new world that appears indifferent to history—with only halls of fame for its champions, chronicles of its big battles, and charts of its greatest hits—accounting for how this digital gamespace came into being presents something of a challenge. Perhaps it is best to approach it in its own style, as a series of levels, each of which appears to the gamer only after you've battled through to the end of the previous one. If you're defeated, you start over. But remember: these are the *grind levels*. The going is hard here, even a little boring. You may need to attempt it more than once. In gamespace, time is measured in discrete and constant units, and while you cannot always win a level, you can always start over and do it again.

[052] CLICK to start. Here is a new world. The first level opens onto a topic (from the Greek "topos," or place). Here a topic is a place both on the ground and within language. Jacques Derrida: "The themes, the topics, the (common-) places, in a rhetorical sense, are strictly inscribed, comprehended each time within a significant site."* One can place one's foot on a topic because one can place one's tongue on it. Or one can point toward it and say: "There it is . . ." All around the topic it is dark, unknown, unmapped, without stories. Move around a bit and you bump into others, from other tribes, other settlements. Via them you learn of still others. The topics start to connect. A map forms. Once there is a map, there is the topographic, which traces lines that connect the topics and which doubles the topical with the space of maps and texts. These outline the contours in space and time of what was the topical, redrawing and rewriting it as a continuous and homogenous plane. The lines of the topic are traced into the page; the lines on the page are traced back onto the earth as topography. History is a story and geography an image of this topography, in which the boundaries are forever being expanded and redrawn. This play between the topical and topographic is the first level.

| theorist | Lukacs | Debord | |
|---|---|---|---|
| auteur | Cooper | Ford | Meier |
| subject | captain | director | manager |
| genre | novel | western | strategy |
| form | book | cinema | game |
| scale | tactics | strategy | logistics |
| line | trail | telegraph | internet |
| ethos | myth | storyline | gamespace |
| topos | topical | topographic | topological |

Fig. C

IN THE first level, every topical feature that resists inscrip- [053] tion as a continuous space is erased and replaced. Impass-able mountains yield their passages, joining once separate topics. Every recalcitrant people with its own indigenous topos is exterminated and forgotten. James Fenimore Cooper: "In a short time there will be no remains of these extraordinary people, in those regions in which they dwelt for centuries, but their names." The names persist, on maps, or in books with titles like *The Last of the Mohicans*. The first level is this dissolution of the topical into the topographic, where an oral lore is erased and replaced by inscription: lines on maps, lines on pages, lines that evolve from trail to rail. The first level is where the topographic unfolds as the line between what is charted and what is uncharted (see Fig. C). The storyline dwells between the

autonomy of the topical and the authority of the topographical, always lagging behind.*

[054]    IN THE cinema, mapping and writing meet. The emergence
of the topographic and its struggle to subsume the topical
becomes the great theme of the American Western genre,
above all in the work of director John Ford. Jimmy Stewart,
the frontier lawyer, bringing the Wild West to book, runs
up against the outlaw gunslinger Lee Marvin. When Stewart shoots him in a showdown, Stewart becomes a legend
and a senator. Only it was John Wayne, the honorable outlaw, who really fired the fatal shot. In *The Man Who Shot
Liberty Valance*, cinema functions as the form that can reveal retrospectively the workings of topography, its creation of a storyline that justifies the imposition of the thin
blue line of the law. The completion of the topographic is
the subject of film noir. Here the topographic has connected all of space in a loose network, and one cannot
run beyond the frontier to escape it. One escapes within,
looking for ill-lit, interstitial topics, like the rail yards and
wholesale markets of Jules Dassin's *Thieves' Highway*. Here,
on the *wrong side of the tracks*, there are still situations for
illicit desire, and an escape from boredom.

[055]    WHAT CLOSES the frontier for free action is the enclosure of
the space of movement within a space of communication.
The line splits—into one that moves objects and subjects,
and into another, faster one that moves information, the
line of telesthesia, of the telegraph then telephone.* In the
western *High Noon*, Sheriff Gary Cooper learns through

the telegraph that his lawless nemesis is arriving on the midday train. In the film noir *The Naked City*, this power of telesthesia—perception at a distance—is everywhere. The police, forensics, the coroner are all brought together via the switchboard operator, enabling and overcoming a division of labor with the telephone and compacting space into a temporal event. We see the policeman make a call, the operator making the connection, and the call being answered. Telesthesia allows the speeding up and coordination of movement along all other lines, setting the railway timetables by which vast armies of goods or soldiers may be mobilized. Telesthesia makes possible the completion of topographic space, where vast territories are coordinated within the bounds of the line. As telesthesia develops, from telegraph to telephone to television to telecommunications, topographic space deepens and hardens but always with gaps and exclusions. Film noir dwells in a gap between the free act in an unmarked space and the imposition of the line. You can run but you can't hide.

EVENTUALLY, even the out-of-the-way topic within the topo- 〖056〗 graphic is mapped and storied. In Dassin's *Night and the City*, made in political exile in London, the whole of space has become telegraphic. There is no escape. This completes the first level. Topology begins when the topical ceases to have any autonomy, when the line along which communication flows closes the gap between map and territory. The open frontier is enclosed in a field of calculation. History and geography cease to dwell between the topical and the topographical, always rushing to keep up.

History and geography are subsumed within a topology, which tends toward a continuous field of equivalent and exchangeable values, instantly communicable everywhere. Where the topical was once bounded within the lines of the topographical, it is now connected along the lines of the topological. The fixed geometry of topography gives way to the variable forms of topology, in which the lines connecting points together lend themselves to transformation without rupture from one shape to another. The storyline of outward movement is complete; the game-space of interior play commences. Welcome to the second level.

[057] **FILM NOIR** comes to an end when it is no longer possible to imagine anything but evil lurking out of bounds. Now if something passes undetected for any length of time it is because it has no value. The era of the great openly declared villains is over. In topological times, the bad guys pass as normal or they corrupt the law. Cinema as the machine for imagining the open space outside the line is consigned to the past. Topology announces its new ambitions through radio and particularly television, a signal for everywhere and nowhere, potentially interested in anyone or anywhere, a *Candid Camera*. The key genres for working out the subsumption of the topographic into the topological are the situation comedy and the game show. On a game show, anyone can be taken out of everyday life and brought into the magic circle of television; on a sitcom, television can extend itself to the everyday life familiar to

the *average viewer,* anywhere. Sitcom and game show announce the coming of a topology in which all of space
might be doubled simultaneously, without lag, by lines of
image, lines of sound, which as yet still broadcast out of
central nodes. The lines run only one way and indiscrimi-
nately but incorporate anyone and anything of value. What
is excluded, from its point of view, has no value. The ro-
mance of the outsider is dead.

WHAT COMPLETES topology and prepares it for the next—   [058]
unknown—level is when the line splits again, into analog
and digital. The analog lines of radio and telephone and
television give way to digital lines, which reach back to the
precedent of the telegraph but extend its digital code to an
increasingly flexible and all-embracing web of communication lines. Gradually, the digital extends and expands to
the whole of telesthesia. The internet incorporates text,
sound, images, then moving images. The cyberspace of
the internet becomes portable and turns into the cellspace
of mobile telephony. This combination of the speed of
telesthesia with the digital code is what makes possible a
vast and inclusive topology of gamespace. This is the third
level: The world of topology is the world of The Cave. Any
and every space is a network of lines, pulsing with digital
data, on which players act and react. In work and play, it is
not the novel, not cinema, not television that offers the line
within which to grasp the form of everyday life, it is the
game. Julian Dibbell: "In the strange new world of imma-
teriality toward which the engines of production have long

been driving us, we can now at last make out the contours of a more familiar realm of the insubstantial—the realm of games and make believe."*

[059] **IF THE** novel, cinema, or television can reveal through their particulars an allegory of the world that makes them possible, the game reveals something else. For the reader, the novel produces allegory as something textual. The world of possibility is the play of the linguistic sign. For the cineaste, the world of possibility is a play of light and shade. For the gamer, the game produces allegory as something algorithmic. The world of possibility is the world internal to the algorithm. So: a passage, mediated by the novel, from the topic to the topographic; a passage, mediated by television, from the topographic to the topological; a passage, mediated by the game, from the topological to as yet unknown spaces, a point where the gamer seems to be stuck. Is it really the case that the gamer merely revels in "blood, mischief and role playing"? Or is there a deeper understanding of the cave that can be had from gaming within it?

[060] **START** over with another new world. (This time with a little gamer theory.) Welcome to the first level: The novel is a line of a certain type, which opens toward certain possibilities, a storyline. It arises at the moment when topic gives way to topography. For literary theorist Georg Lukács, what is to be valued is the historical novel and its ability to trace a line across an historical moment and reveal the forces at

work in it. "It is the portrayal of the broad living basis of historical events in their intricacy and complexity, in their manifold interaction with acting individuals."* The historical novel shows historical events through secondary characters, perhaps not unlike the reader, and a historical event as being at the same time a transformation of everyday life. And yet the novel suffers from this paradox: To illuminate the topographic, the novel has to hide its own form. If it explores the possibilities of the line within its pages, it opens itself to a "formalism" that leaves the reader behind.

**THE FIRST** level continues: Cinema is a line of a certain type, which opens toward certain possibilities, an illumination of the dark corners of topography. For screen theorist Walter Benjamin, what is to be valued is the "optical unconscious," cinema's machinic vision of a world that is itself machined with a dense grid of lines. Cinema can expand or shrink space, extend or compress time, it can cut together images of diverse scales or forms—intimations of topology. It creates a "Spielraum," a playroom, for dividing up the machine world otherwise. Contra Lukács, Benjamin opens toward the formal properties of the line at the expense of its representation of a historical situation as a totality. But what doesn't change is that the spectator, like the reader, is external to the line itself. Cinema can show how the world is made through its cuts and montages, an industrial process with the unique quality of showing itself as it works. Yet there is still a separation between those making the cinema and those watching it.

[061]

[062] **THE FIRST** level ends: The novel languishes. Cinema fails to realize its allegorical potential. Theorist and practitioner of anti-cinema Guy Debord: "But this life and this cinema are both equally paltry; and that is why you could actually exchange one for the other with indifference."* Boredom reigns.

[063] **THE SECOND** level begins: Radio is a line of a certain type, which opens toward certain possibilities. For Bertolt Brecht, what is to be valued in it is a certain unrealized potential for the line to point both ways: "Radio is one-sided and it should be two. It is purely an apparatus for distribution, for mere sharing out. So here is a positive suggestion: change this apparatus over from distribution to communication. The radio would be the finest possible communication apparatus in public life, a vast network of pipes. That is to say, it would be if it knew how to receive as well as transmit, how to let the listener speak as well as hear, how to bring him into a relationship instead of isolating him."* Radio could be like a public telephony. But it is all analog flow; it lacks a digital code. It radiates from one point to every other, without distinction. It lacks the transformational geometry of topology, where any three specific points could be connected, anywhere, and still make the same "triangle" connecting sender and receiver and the third "line"—space itself.

[064] **THE SECOND** level continues. Television expands the line of radio, but does it add much to it? Does it yield much by way of a space of possibility? Fredric Jameson: "The block-

age of fresh thinking before this solid little window against which we strike our heads being not unrelated to precisely that whole or total flow we observe through it."* Television generalizes the line of communication as an analog flow. The digital has not yet prevailed.

THE SECOND level ends: The tension between the topo-   [0b5]
graphic and topological is also one between a declining sphere of representation, will, and interest, and one of a new topos that is statistical, digital, simulated—algorithmic. The topographic is incomplete. It can project its lines across space and annihilate time, but it cannot effectively mark or measure out the space it encloses. It has some feeble mechanisms—the opinion poll, for example. Through the laborious means of seeking out and recording opinion, topological space can be given the appearance of agency. Jean Baudrillard: "It is, paradoxically, as a game that the opinion polls recover a sort of legitimacy. A game of the undecideable; a game of chance . . . Perhaps we can see here the apparition of one of these collective forms of the game that Caillois called *alea*—an irruption into the polls themselves of a ludic, aleatory process, an ironic mirror for the use of the masses."*

THE THIRD level begins. Where the topographic develops   [0bb]
one dimension of telegraphy—its flow of information across space—the topological develops the other—its intricate coding and addressing. Where the topographic is an analog flow, the topological is the digital divide. It is a line of another type. It is a line that, for a brief, burning mo-

ment, reignited the dreams of a new topos. But the cycle accelerates. If it took twenty years to get from Brecht or Benjamin's optimism to Debord's boredom, the same cycle in net time took perhaps five years. Cyber theorist Geert Lovink: "Cyberspace at the dawn of the 21st century can no longer position itself in a utopian void of seamless possibilities."* What topology yields is not a cyberspace but a gamespace. The idea of cyberspace is still too linked to images from the world of radio and television, of flow and "seamless" movement, of access and excess, of lines running anywhere and everywhere. Topology is experienced more as a gamespace than a cyberspace: full of restrictions and hierarchies, firewalls and passwords. It is more like a bounded game than a free space of play. Once again: If it is free, it is valueless. Those odd lines within topology where anything goes are the ones of no consequence.

[067] THE THIRD level continues. Games have storylines like the historical novel, which arc from beginning to end. Games have cinematic cut scenes, pure montages of attraction. Games subsume the lines of television just as television subsumed cinema and cinema the novel. But they are something else as well. They are not just an allegory but a double form, an allegory and an allegorithm. Appearances within the game double an algorithm which in turn simulates an unknown algorithm which produces appearances outside the game. So far so good. But where gamer theory gets stuck is in the tension between thinking games through the forms of the past and the desire

to found a—somewhat hasty—claim to a new "field" or "topic" of scholarship around some "new media." Is the game about story or play? Is the authoritative method "narratology" or "ludology"? Questions too ill-framed to answer. The question of the form of the game cannot be separated from the question of the form of the world—of gamespace. Boredom reigns again.

START over. Another new world. Welcome to the first level. [068] Let's loop back to Lukács and ask: Rather than insist on the possibilities of the technicity of the line itself, perhaps there's something to be said for the possibilities of a certain genre that makes use of it? Bonus points! Skip straight to the third level: The strategy game is a genre of a certain type within a line of a certain type, which opens toward certain possibilities. Click on the Government pulldown menu and choose Revolution. Your Republic turns to Anarchy. Certain parameters shift. You are playing *Sid Meier's Civilization III.** It is not so much an allegory for world history as an allegorithm for gamespace itself. Everything here is a relation between quantifiable processes. Everything is a question of the allocation of resources. There's a perverse sense of base and superstructure. You can change the form of Government but there's not much you can do to change the underlying form of production. Invest in science, and qualitative technical changes accumulate, which in turn expand military, cultural, and political possibilities. Invest in culture to keep the plebs from revolting. Civil disorder comes from below, while revolutions come from above, but these are just two functions within an algorithm: a small variable with a big effect; a big variable with a small effect.

[069] **GAMESPACE** turns descriptions into a database, and storyline into navigation. Sid Meier, known as a voracious reader, turns history and anthropology books into strategy games. *Civilization III* (designed by others, but in his style) even comes with its own *Civilopedia,* a reference work for a parallel world. But this is more than the remediation of old forms into new. Rather, the algorithm consumes the topographic and turns it into the topological. In the database, all description is numerical, equivalent in form. In principle everything within it can be related to or transformed into everything else. A new kind of symmetry operates. The navigation of the database replaces a narration via description. The database expands exponentially. Rather than a politics of allegory, an economics of allegorithm operates, selecting and reducing possibilities.

[070] **THIS IS** how the world appears to a gamer playing *Civilization III:* There are dependent and independent variables. Gamers, through trial and error, work out which are which. They change over time. In the first stage, you explore, pushing back the inky black shroud to make a map. Then you grow the population, a vast army of farmers and miners. You have to maximize useable space. Once your continent fills up with cities and their hinterlands, expansion becomes qualitative rather than quantitative. It's all

about knowledge and technology. The quality of warfare changes along the way. It expands in space, digs deeper into reserves of resources, then becomes a qualitative race for bigger and better lines along which power can reticulate. The gamer is a manager, confronting uncertainty with an inventory of resources. It's a hard game to win at first, but after you have beaten it, you play it again and again. Gamer theorist Glen Fuller: "It has a complex array of logics for warding off boredom." It draws the gamer's attention not to the storyline but to the combinations of elements from which any given storyline might be selected.

IN *CIVILIZATION III*, time is essentially of a piece. It is homogenous, empty, but it can be divided into equivalent units, just like space. Thus time can be configured and reconfigured, producing endless variations on the cascading sequences of cause and effect. History is indeed absent from the game, absent as something finished, as a storyline in the past tense. What replaces it is a history workshop, a model of history as the intuition of algorithms and their consequences. The gamer is a designer. Designers, like all managers, operate within given limits. This is how the world appears to the game designer: There are dependent and independent variables. Designers, through trial and error, will work out which are which. They will choose cultural, business, and technical options that maximize long-term advantages. If it doesn't work out, they will do it over. Time is essentially of a piece. It is homogenous, but it can be divided into equivalent units. *Civi-*

*lization III* models not so much "civilization" as the game-design business, which in turn models gamespace, or topology as it presently exists.

[072] THIS IS how the world appears to gamer theory: Seen from the point of view of topology, with its dense databases and navigating tools, the topical world with its loosely connected topics was a world of limited data and few possibilities. Transformations of one thing into another were purely magical. The topographic—and telegraphic—flattened out the differences between topics while describing them in much more detail. A tension arises between enriched description and the poverty of storyline, bursting to contain it. The expansion of description nevertheless opened toward allegory. Accumulations of images burst out of their storyline bounds. It opened toward a politics of allegory, of the writing and mapping of the world, and also toward utopia, arresting the flux of the world in ideal form. Topology closes the frontiers of space within its lines and expands the dataset again, but by reducing data to equivalent calculable points it is able to break with storyline as the principle of temporal order, replacing it with the algorithm. Storyline becomes gamespace.

[073] STRATEGY games such as *Civilization III* present an allegorithm of topology as gamespace and the gamer as its manager. It subsumes text, audio, images, and movies into the database, while the algorithm calculates the moves of all its elements relative to the gamer. It collapses the difference between the everyday and the utopian. It embraces

all differences by rendering all of space and time as quantifiable. Topical times resound with the myth of the tactician. Topographic times inscribe stories of grand directors of strategy. Topological times call for managers of logistics. History appears, retrospectively, as not only the expanding frontier of war's theatre but also its qualitative transformation. It is the unwinding of a line which divides everything into manageable chunks of data. The actual disposition of resources is doubled by a database which maps not fixed locations but measures of fungibility. The algorithm can produce every possible combination of the resources mapped in the database—and a few impossible ones as well. The possible and the actual reverse positions. It is the possible that is real. If the algorithm can produce it as an outcome from the database, it exists. The mystery is why the recalcitrant debris that litters the actual sometimes refuses to get out of the way. This insistence on the reality of the possible, on what resides within resources, is the American dream. The debris of the real portends its latent destiny.

FINALLY, the next level appears: the expansion of topology [074] outward, beyond America, to make America equivalent to all of time and space. America itself, as a construct, as a structure of feeling, is always only available via particular mediating lines, which may do more than merely represent a pre-existing America. The form of the line may itself participate in the creation of America.* There may well be an America that resides successively in the novel, in the cinema, in television, and in the game, and is shaped by each. Each, in turn, presents history itself as a passing on of memory from one form to another. *Civilization III* recapitulates not only world history but media history, the history of media as form. Its ambition is not only to embrace the recording of the world but the world of recording. In *Civilization III,* the transformation of space and time, from topic to topography to topology, is an effect of the development of the lines with which to mark and manage it. This double development, which at one and the same time deepens and proliferates lines of the possible and the actual, can be called America. It is what is both desired and feared under the rubric of that name, which no longer marks a particular topic but stands for the very capacity to mark and manage space itself, as topology. When playing *Civilization III,* it doesn't matter if the civilization you choose to play is Babylon or China, Russia or Zululand, France or India. Whoever wins is America, in that the logic of the game itself is America. America unbound.

[075] THE LINE makes its way across the world, making it by marking it. The line passes across valleys, pages, mountains, rivers, tracing trails, roads, railways, highways, doubling itself with telegraph, television, telecommunications, doubling itself again as the code of the letter migrates from text to telegraph and explodes into the myriad lines of the digital. The line makes topics, maps them into the topographic, then folds the topographic into a digital topology. The line does something else as well. For every line drawn there are an infinite number undrawn. Every line is an allegory of the possibilities for a line of its type. The line may

also intimate the possibilities of lines to come. But the possibilities of a given type of line are not infinite. Allegory always touches the virtual—which one might define as the possibility of possibility—via a particular line. At each level of the actual unfolding of the line across the world, it offers a glimpse of the virtual in its own image. This is the limit to allegory. If allegory yearns for something ahistorical, a topos beyond all particulars, it does so over and over in the most particular and mediated way.

# ANALOG

(on *Katamari Damacy*)

SISYPHUS, FOUNDER of Corinth, father of Odysseus, founder of the Ismithian Games, is best known for a most cruel and unusual punishment, meted out to him by the Gods. He was to roll a huge stone up the mountainside, watch helplessly as it rolled back down again, and then start all over again. Nobody knows what he did that required such a punishment. Perhaps it was for revealing the designs of the Gods to mortals. Revealing the forms beyond the mere particulars of mortal life would, in topical times, be a serious crime. Or perhaps, more prosaically, it was for his habit of murdering seafarers and travelers. Topical space, where each law, each God, is bordered by zones of indifference, would surely be troubled by such a transgression of the rules of "xenia," of the gift one owes to strangers. Anne Carson: "The characteristic features of xenia, namely its basis in reciprocation and its assumption of perpetuity, seem to have woven a texture of personal alliances that held the ancient world together." Or so it was in topical times.*

[077] IN TOPOGRAPHIC times, Sisyphus is a hero. He revels in this new world from which the Gods and their intangible forms have fled and a great industrial engine usurps their place. The task of Sisyphus becomes everyone's labor: pointless, repetitive, endless, shoulder to the wheel of fortune. There are no longer any lawless spaces. There are no gaps between topics. All of space is within the law. There are no more border zones where indifference prevails. Certainly it gets much harder to get away with murdering travelers. But in topographic times, it is time itself that is not quite so completely subordinated to rules, to ends, to purposes. There is a limit to the working day, and even within the working day not every second is called to account. Albert Camus: "I leave Sisyphus at the foot of the mountain! One always finds one's burden again. But Sisyphus teaches the higher fidelity that negates the Gods and raises rocks. He too concludes that all is well. This universe henceforth without a master seems to him neither sterile nor futile. Each atom of that stone, each mineral flake of that night-filled mountain, in itself forms a world."* The topical Sisyphus played fast and loose with the gaps of space, between the topics; the topographic Sisyphus played in the gaps of time and exploited those gaps to turn everything to account for himself alone.

[078] WHERE IS Sisyphus now? Using the analog sticks on the game controller, you move a little character who rolls a ball

| topical | topographic | topological |
|---------|-------------|-------------|
| analog > digital | analog & digital | analog < digital |
| Homer's Odyssey | Myth of Sisyphus | Katamari Damacy |

Fig. D

called a Katamari. The game is called *Katamari Damacy.** The name translates roughly as "clump spirit," which might in turn translate as "analog." As the Katamari ball rolls, things stick to it. At first it is small things that stick, household items picked up off the living room floor. The ball gets bigger as things stick, and so it can pick up bigger things. Once your ball is big enough, you move out of the house and into the world. To move the ball, you twizzle the little analog joysticks. Push the sticks forward, and the character rolls the ball forward. Pull the sticks back and the character rolls the ball back. Turn left, turn right—it feels as though the variable pressure on the sticks translates into variable movements. This is analog—a relation of continuous variation. Only it isn't really. It is a digital game. The game converts the continuous movement of your thumbs on the sticks into a digital code. It turns movements into decisions—back/forwards, left/right, stop/start. An algorithm calculates the outcome of each movement. If you roll your ball over a small object, you pick it up. If you roll your ball over one that is too big, you collide with it, throwing off a few things you have already gathered. Analog spirit becomes digital code (see Fig. D).

[079] **ALL GAMES** are digital. Without exception. They all come down to a strict decision: out or in, foul or fair, goal or no goal. Anything else is just "play." Jesper Juul: "The affinity between computers and games is one of the ironies of human history." But not at all surprising. From the start, games were a proto-computer—machines assembled out of human motion, inanimate materials, and the occasional dubious call by the referee. Sisyphus is condemned to a useless labor which is at the same time useless play, in that it cannot bring about a decision. The rock he rolls never crosses a line. It rolls right past the notional top of the mountain and overshoots the bottom of its own momentum. It is not an algorithm because it can never end. But in *Katamari Damacy*, things are different. Rather than the rolling of the ball being entirely useless, now it is entirely purposeful. Time, like space, no longer harbors indifference. Brenda Laurel: "Even the smallest fragments of your idle time have been colonized." As you roll your ball around, making it bigger and bigger, an icon in the corner of the screen shows your progress. The icon shows your ball as a circle inside a larger one, which is the size it must grow to if you are to win this level. It grows, gradually, incrementally, but at some point—a decision. Big enough! An analog progression stops at the digital threshold.*

[080] **HERE IS** a version of the Katamari myth: You are a Prince sent down to earth by a careless King who in a moment of boredom got drunk and destroyed the heavens. The Katamari balls you roll up are offerings to him. If your ball is big enough, he uses it to replace one of the stars he

trashed in the sky. The King then sets for the Prince the task of rolling up a bigger one. Perhaps this storyline is an allegory for the relation that holds now between the analog and the digital. The twizzling of the sticks on the controller, the rolling up of the balls on the screen, is the task demanded by gamespace—a task that gamespace can only recognize by rewarding the gamer with a score. Topology, with its endless, intricate lines—wireless, satellite, fiber optic—turns anything and everything into a meaningless smear of data. Gamespace installs itself in topology to reduce that smear to a decision, a yes, a no, a straight line, and to convey back to the gamer the result of the gamer's actions. The analog is now just a way of experiencing the digital. The decision on whether something can appear or not appear is digital. You and your character the Prince are confined to the analog, rolling from topic to topic. The King commands the digital heavens. He decides what point in the sky each ball is to occupy.

IN THE myth of Sisyphus the task is to roll the ball to the top without quite knowing where the top is. There's no mark, no point, no code. Sisyphus pushes the ball up, but it either falls short or falls over the unmarked peak and rolls back down again. In the game of Katamari there is no such ambiguity. Each threshold is clearly marked. The analog movement of rolling the ball, continuously increasing its size, takes place within the given limits of the digital. There is an exact mark at which it flips from being too small to just the right size. The reign of topology subordinates the analog to the digital. Where once analog and dig-

[081]

ital maintained an ambiguous and continuous—analog—relation to each other and to the world, the digital now distinguishes itself sharply from the analog, subsuming the analog difference under the digital distinction. This is a transformation not merely in forms of communication or entertainment, not even in forms of power or of topos, but a change in being itself. The digital appears, finally, to install topology in the world—except in the process it has installed the world within topology. In *Katamari Damacy,* the world is just stuff, there for the clumping. It is King Digital's decision on its name, size, and place in the heavens that gives it being.

[082] THE SCREEN in *Katamari Damacy* shows a clock in the corner, an old-fashioned analog disk with a sweeping hand. The game is an allegorithm of a double process—by which the analog movements of the gamer are transformed into the digital but also by which the digital decisions of the game are expressed to the gamer in a familiar analog form. Gamespace subordinates all of time and space to the digital. Paul Virilio: "Space had been measured, mapped, time has become clock time, the diversity of relief, of topography, gave way to topology."* In topographic times the clocktower showed its face to the town over which it presided; now time is blinking digits, seen anywhere and everywhere. Just check your cell phone. The hands of the analog clock turn time into movement in space, reducing it to a line that rotates on a plane. The digital clock substitutes one coded sign for another, at fixed intervals, drawing each from an abstract space where all the signs of the

code exist outside of time. All of time becomes a series of discrete, equivalent, and interchangeable units. At each interval, time can be arrested and made to yield a number. Where the analog temporalized space, now the digital spatializes time.

TWIST the sticks on the controller, and on the screen the [083] Prince turns the ball. Roll the ball, and it gradually grows as it picks things up. The analog icon in the corner grows as the ball grows. One movement doubles another. The analog records, in this measuring continuum, how several movements, operating together, produce a transformation. It tracks the movement of rolling the ball, a movement that continuously transforms itself out of itself. The analog is all about relations. The digital is all about boundaries. The digital does not follow a moving line; it imposes a grid of lines that function as thresholds. The line at which the ball is deemed big enough is imposed by King Digital. In the analog, difference is a productivity in excess of itself; in the digital, distinction is a negation that comes from outside of time. Roll the ball as much as you like, but unless it reaches the size King Digital demands within the time he allows, you fail—and are subjected to his lofty disdain. This is the limit to movement that appears time and time again.

THE ANALOG is variation along a line, a difference of [084] more—and less. The digital is divided by a line, a distinction between either/or. Either the ball clumps enough stuff to be a star or it doesn't. The analog may vary along more than one line at once, producing the appearance of a qualitative difference. The digital introduces a code, which may produce complex relations among its terms, but all the terms are separated by the same line of absolute distinction. All the Katamari balls that are big enough become stars, each with its own name and location, but all are points in the same heavens. In this digital cosmos, everything is of the same substance. Nothing is really qualitatively different. A cow, a car, your cousin: each has its shape and color, but in the end it's all the same, just stuff. In *Katamari Damacy* it is mostly consumer stuff, but this goes far beyond a critique of the commodity. Topology can make infinite digital distinctions. It is all just bits, and all bits are equivalent. The digital separates everything into discrete segments by imposing a universal code that allows anything to be connected to anything else—topology—but prevents anything from ever being different. The cosmos of difference is what King Digital has lost, and what he commands his gamer Prince to replace with a cosmos composed of mere distinctions.

〖085〗 THE ANALOG may move backward or forward along a line, or even track movement across three or more dimensions; but only with the imposition of the digital code is it possible to cut the terms bounded by the digital line and rearrange them. Rather than an analog movement through space and time, the digital opens the possibility of jumping between points in a space outside of time in which terms are arrayed along different axes and are drawn together via the code. Rather than a continuous line moving out from a point into a three-dimensional space, one imagines rather a three-dimensional space of fixed points, which can be called upon by the code to make up a straight line of distinct units. Because it is digital, the game can be "saved." After you have successfully rolled a ball, you can save it. Saving takes place at the digital threshold. The digital creates a timeless space that can be saved by making all of time equivalent. It is a time without violence. What is saved does not suffer from erosion or decomposition or decay. It always comes back as the same—unless the system crashes and the digital can no longer impose its code, in which case it may never come back at all. The digital cosmos is more perfect, yet so much more fragile. It is the realm of Plato's forms made concrete and saved to disk.

AS THE Prince rolls bigger and bigger balls, he gets to play [086] in a bigger and bigger topos. The game starts inside an apartment, then moves on to the town and finally to the world. This stepping up through bigger and bigger scales repeats the stepping up through the scales of the topical, the topographic and the topological of which the game is an allegorithm. What gives the game its charm is the seemingly ridiculous idea that a ball of household items could be a star. Even more odd: the last and largest ball replaces the smallest heavenly body—a mere moon. But this is of a piece with the ways of topology. In topological times, it is not just that the digital now operates on a planetary scale. It is that it operates across scales, connecting the infinitesimal to the gigantic. The tiniest switch of electric current can launch a cruise missile. Form is detached from scale.

[087] KING DIGITAL destroyed the heavens, in a moment of boredom, in a fit of indifference. This is the danger of topology.
Indifference is no longer something that lurks merely in
the margins of space or time. Having been squeezed more
and more to the margin of both space and time, rather
than disappearing, indifference threatens to become total,
pervasive, immanent. The Prince is what the Prince has
achieved—a level, a number, and nothing but. Julian
Stallabrass: "Emotional attachment to the game is established through labor, emerging out of the Sisyphean nature of the player's task."* For all his laid-back style, King
Digital makes a terrible demand, as appalling as that made
of Sisyphus by the Gods. He commands the gamer to the
game, yet promises nothing but victory until defeat. The
only reward is that the very time itself that the gamer com-
mits to the task will make the task worthwhile. The digital
object exists in a space that chunks it into bits, each of
equivalent value. The digital subject also exists in a time
that chunks it into bits, each of equivalent value. This is
the price paid by the gamer to gamespace.

[088] DIGITAL OBJECT, digital subject—these are byproducts of a
boredom that, seeking respite from nothingness, projects
its lines across all space and time, turning it into a topology of commodity space and military space. This is the
reckless act of creation with which *Katamari Damacy* begins—the King's destruction of the mythic heaven of the
old Gods, and the project of replacing it by commanding
the transformation of a human, analog movement into an
airless matrix of machine code. This is the new task of Sis-

yphus. Gamespace is always and everywhere the imposition of the digital as a way of laying an invisible hand on the world—or an all-too-visible fist. Where the invisible hand opens its digits to calculate what it may gain, the invisible fist closes them to calculate what it may claim.

THE MILITARY industrial complex developed photography, [089] radar, radio—all the lines of analog telesthesia—as a means of measuring and controlling its forces. This development reached a limit, and its forces exceeded its capacity to manage them. Digital telesthesia—starting perhaps with the SAGE computer system of the 1950s—emerged as the means of command, control, and communication. Paul Edwards: "For SAGE set the key pattern for other high-technology weapon systems, a nested set of increasingly comprehensive military enclosures for global oversight and control." The theory of the digital, and of its distinction from the analog, emerges as a byproduct of this attempt at self-control by the military industrial complex, but it transformed the complex into something else. The expansive movement of the military machine calls into being a code that can monitor and manage it. The analog begets the digital, but only produces the concept of the analog after the fact. Anthony Wilden: "Obviously, without the digital, we could not speak of the analog." Without the recognition of the ball as a putative star, it cannot be named. The military entertainment complex emerges out of the control of the analog by the digital, of the military and industrial production lines by the digital lines of command, and by the extension of the digital to all aspects of everyday life.*

[090] **WITHOUT** the analog, play leaves no trace. Without the digital, play yields no score. Neither analog nor digital is play itself. But what can one say about play? Play is what has to be posited for there to be anything for either the analog or the digital to track, and yet play is an elusive concept at best. Play theorist Brian Sutton-Smith: "We all play occasionally, and we all know what play feels like. But when it comes to making theoretical statements about what play is, we fall into silliness."* Perhaps the very concept of play appears only retrospectively. Obviously, without the analog and the digital, we could not speak of play, even as play exceeds the analog line along which it is traced and the digital line across which it is measured. Via the analog, play is captured in art; via the digital, play is captured in games. The analog flattens play out into a single line, so that its movement may continue, in reduced form, into another space. The play of the fingers on the controller is recorded via the graphic art on the screen. The analog enables a movement to communicate from topos to topos. The digital codifies play, translating it onto the very different space of number and logic—of code.

[091] **WHICH** came first, play or game? Which came first, moves or rules? Sisyphus was interested in both navigation and commerce, at a time when both still had a tenuous map of the spaces through which they plied their ships and their trade. The rules emerged out of the moves. Play produced what, after the fact, could be marked a transgression. Sisyphus transgressed—either by killing another traveler or perhaps by seeking to know the rules of the Gods in ad-

vance. His punishment is an eternal move which can never give rise to a game, which yields no end, no win, no recognition. Now the terms are reversed. Play does not inspire the game; the game animates play. Behind the subordination of the analog to the digital is the subordination of play to game. Tracing the line of the move, the play, matters less than the score it yields, the threshold it crosses. King Digital makes quite the opposite demand of the Prince to that made of Sisyphus by the Gods. The eternal task is no longer the move that can never cross the finish line, it is the move that can do nothing but yield a measure, a score, a number, a rank. Rather than play that can never end, it is the game that stops, and starts, and stops, and starts, and stops, and starts—forever.

THE TERMS analog and digital are invariably treated as if the [092] relation between them was itself a digital one. This is a sign of the times. These terms are to be treated as discrete and absolutely distinct, a code with two absolute terms. Any ambiguity or play that might threaten to deconstruct the distinction is to be resolved with distinctions of an ever-finer resolution. This in turn leads to ever more complexity in managing the proliferation of bits, which in turn requires ever more powerful data-crunching engines. The military entertainment complex discovers experimentally that if the relation between the analog and the digital is digital, an absolute boundary, then the domain of the digital can be perfected as one of purely relative and numerical value—a gamespace. This digital realm can then become the locus for command and control of the analog remainder, which it treats as a mere residue. The lines of the digital can be inscribed ever more extensively and intensively on the world, to the point where a digital heaven is realized, and the analog seems to vanish, and play becomes a mere effect of the digital. The Analog Prince only rolls the ball, steering this way and that, because King Digital commands it. And why does he command it? To make the universe over, to recreate being itself, as an effect of the digital as a command.

[093] THE DIGITAL, once installed in the world, defeats the logic of the storyline within which the digital serves to make the analog manifest, but does not control it. The novel, which from James Fenimore Cooper to William Gibson narrates the rise and fall of the military industrial complex, uses the codes of language to follow a series of movements beyond language's ken. The digital produces not just new kinds of media but a whole new topos, in which the role and rule of the line is reversed. One no longer follows a line to find where it divides; one divides with a line to make a distinction. Storyline becomes gamespace. The storyline that inaugurates the world of *Katamari Damacy* is not a creation myth but a destruction script. The storyline's last task is to erase itself and initiate the new conditions of difference for gamespace. This task—like that of Sisyphus—must be endlessly repeated.

[094] THE DIGITAL, once installed in the world, accelerates the potential for change, but for change always of the same type. The Analog Prince can roll up many things to make his

Katamari balls, but any difference among these objects is lost. All that matters is their aggregation, glommed together as more and more of the same. Likewise, the military entertainment complex grids the earth so it may gird it, making it over in the image of its digital rulings, making it amenable to the imposition of a code of unambiguous stratifications. Distinctions proliferate wildly, beyond the simple dichotomies of the topographic. But these distinctions are always and everywhere exchangeable equivalents within the logistics of commodity space and military space. Roll up more and more balls, populate the heavens with a veritable Milky Way, but each is distinct from the other always in the same way. Drew Milne: "What once ventured forth as processual *mathesis* becomes the reified calculus of administration, a logic of numerical sameness screened from nihilistic relativity."*

THE DIGITAL emerges as military, but achieves acceptance [095] as entertainment. J. C. Herz: "Most of the technology that's now used in videogames had its origins in military research. When you trace back the patents, it's virtually impossible to find an arcade or console component that evolved in the absence of a Defense Department grant."* The military versions of digital telesthesia make the world over as a military space, but the digital does not yet become a culture other than for a small band of specialists tied to the military industrial complex. The coming together of the digital and the entertainment commodity inscribes the digital not just in space and time but in cultural perceptions of space and time.

[096] THE DIGITAL game is a very particular commodity. It is not just the usual store of entertaining representations transferred from analog and mechanical reproduction to a digital form. Rather, it makes the digital itself into entertainment. The digital always addresses its subject as a gamer, a manager, a calculator and competitor who has value only in relation to a mark, a score. The digital inscribes gamespace within the subject itself. Gamespace makes topology seem like it could have, if not meaning, then at least an algorithm. Gamespace makes the uploading of the world into topology seem natural and inevitable. Yet at the same time it offers the digital in its purest form, where the transformation of analog into digital is always consistent, repeatable—in a word, fair. While the game makes the digital seem inescapable, its ambiguity is in the way it also makes the digital seem like it could be an atopian realm. The game naturalizes gamespace, and yet calls it to account as inadequate in its own terms.

[097] THE DIGITAL makes the analog itself appear as something distinct. The digital rules a line between analog and digital, making a slippery difference into a clear distinction. But perhaps, having made the distinction appear, the perspective can be reversed, and the digital can be perceived from the point of view of its analog residue. What might emerge is rather the play between the analog and the digital. The digital might become again the threshold that turns a movement into a break, rather than imposing the break on movement. The gamer as theorist might look toward a transformation of what matters within gamespace, a style of play that edges away from agon, distinction, decision,

the fatal either/or. Because after a while it's just no fun. Johan Huizinga: "And undoubtedly the predominance of the agonistic principle does lead to decadence in the long run."*

"I DON'T play games," says Keita Takahashi, designer of [098] *Katamari Damacy.* He is a sculptor. "I am happy going through this game phase of my life, where I can get paid and eat."* As the digital subsumes the analog, so too the designer subsumes the artist. The longing to return to art as an analog pursuit—the trace of the hand in clay or paint—may be in vain. But the artist within the designer may still inscribe the analog in the heart of the digital as something irreducible. The artist is now the insider who finds a new style of trifling within the game. The artist as outsider is dead, for there is no outside from which to signal back across the border. The limit to the game has to be found from within. The Analog Prince is the very figure of the artist in topological times, who plays gamely, twisting this way and that on the controls, managing to get out into bigger and bigger spaces, but always unable to escape gamespace.

KING Digital may rule in *Katamari Damacy,* but it is his [099] subordinate, the Prince, upon whose labors this digital topology is built. Not the least of the charms of Takahashi's work is this foregrounding of the labor the gamer performs. It is no longer labor as punishment for defying the Gods. It is no longer absurd labor, performed consciously and joyously in spite of the absence of the Gods. Topology installs, in place of the absent Gods, King Digital, and his demand that, while labor is punishingly hard and absurdly pointless, it nevertheless has its measure. Sisyphus, the Analog Prince, labors to roll up everything in this world-made-over under the mark of the digital and offer it up for appraisal. What the digital has always wanted—to be the form of all forms—has come to pass. Our punishment for attempting to steal those forms for our own purposes is to labor endlessly to repeat them. *Katamari Damacy* extends the atopia of the digital to the heavens themselves.

[100] WHEN the Prince manages to complete a level, *Katamari Damacy* rewards the gamer with a cut scene, a short animation about the Hoshino family. They are cute but rather chunky, as if the digital had already snapped them to its grid. The Hoshinos watch their astronaut father Tomio as he begins his voyage to the Moon. Tomio's mission is canceled because there is no Moon to which to travel. The last mission of the game, "Make the Moon," requires rolling up most of the objects on Earth, including the Hoshino family and their father's rocket. Once the Prince has restored the Moon to the King's satisfaction, a final cut scene shows the Hoshino family—mother and father, boy and girl—on the new Moon. Having completed the reconstruction of the cosmos as one of digital distinctions rather than analog differences, a digital people find themselves already there, already inhabiting the Moon to which Tomio was to travel. There is no need to travel—that great pastime of topographic times. Now there's no place to go that is not subject to the same code. The reign of King Digital, the King of All Cosmos, is complete.*

# ATOPIA

(on *Vice City*)

I T'S LIKE PARADISE HERE. Everything [101] seems pastel-hued as you drive by, with the radio on. The car is stolen, but so long as the police didn't see you it won't matter. You don't really have to be anywhere or do anything. The hotels and condos are comfortable and discreet. If you need money, mug some-one. The body makes a satisfyingly squishy sound when you kick it. There are adventures. You get to meet some interesting people. It is a city of gangsters, hustlers, and honeys. It's all tourism, drugs, guns, cars, and personal services. Nobody makes anything, except maybe "ice cream," porn, and counterfeit money. Everybody buys, sells, or steals. *Vice City* is a nice place. It is not quite utopia. And nor is it some dark dystopia. There's no storyline here, where paradise turns nasty, in which the telling early detail turns out to be a clue to the nightmare beneath the surface, the severed ear of *Blue Velvet*. Without the possibility of dystopia, there's no utopia either. Terry Eagleton: "All utopian writing is also dystopian, since, like Kant's sublime, it cannot help reminding us of our mental limits in the act of striving to go beyond them." In *Vice City* there is no "beyond." As one would expect in a high-end land of vice, its offer is *all-inclusive*.*

[102] IN GAMESPACE, the very possibility of utopia is foreclosed.* It is no longer possible to describe a shining city upon the hill, as if it were a special topic untouched by the everyday, workaday world. No space is sacred; no space is separate. Not even the space of the page. The gamelike extends its lines everywhere and nowhere. And yet, a pure digital game like *Vice City* might still perform some curious, critical function. Why do so many choose to escape from their everyday gamespace into yet more games? As the myriad lines of topology work their way into space, space mutates, and just as the allegorical moment changes from the topical to the topographic to the topological, so too does the utopian moment. One might think gamespace via both allegory (doubled as allegorithm) and utopia (mutated into atopia). One reveals which could be, the other announcing what should be, both shifting and realigning as the space around us changes what it would be.

[103] UTOPIA was a place to hide, where a topic could develop of its own accord, safe within the bounds of the book. There, life could begin again outside of conflict. Utopias do their best to expel violence. In a utopian text there is always a

barrier in space (distant and difficult terrain) or a barrier in time (intervening revolutions or Charles Fourier's cycles of epochs). But the real barrier is that troublesome line that divides what is on the page from what is outside it. Fredric Jameson: "I believe that we can begin from the proposition that Utopian space is an imaginary enclave within real social space, in other words, that the very possibility of Utopian space is itself a result of spatial and social differentiation." Except that utopia's enclave was not imaginary. It was tangible and material. Utopia is a place on a page where violence is pushed to the margin by the power of sheer description. Utopian socialist William Morris: "Success in besting our neighbors is a road to renown now closed."*

UTOPIA restricted itself to a particular topic (the topic of the page) and a particular line (the line of writing). The book is a line—a trajectory, a connection through time and space with certain qualities (see Fig. E). Among its qualities is the way it partitions off the smooth space of the page from the rough-and-tumble world without. It rules off from the world that special tempo where text plays its subtle games against its reader. In a utopia, other lines of communication are either nonexistent or subordinated to the descriptive power of the text. Utopian Communist A. A. Bogdanov: "The plays were either transmitted from distant large cities by means of audio visual devices, or—more usually—they were cinematic reproductions of plays performed long ago, sometimes so long ago that the actors themselves were already dead."* In this utopian *Red Star,*

| topical | topographic | topological |
|---------|-------------|-------------|
| utopia/dystopia | heterotopia | atopia |
| More's *Utopia* | Perec's *W* | *Vice City* |

Fig. E

the new lines extend and enhance those of the text, rather than supersede them.

[105]   IT IS not that utopias alone create gulags. Adolf Eichmann was no utopian. He just kept the trains running on time—to the camps. His was a prosaic imagination, making topography match the text of his orders. The lines for implementing that kind of violence are the railway line, the telegraph line, and the line of punch cards passing through the tabulators—precursors to the digital computer. Holocaust historian Edwin Black: "When Germany wanted to identify the Jews by name, IBM showed them how."* In topography there is a whole nest of connections, along which flows information, radiating from the text, calling the world to order. There are lines for planning, managing, measuring. Topography is not only the means of producing spatial and social differentiation but of overcoming it, connecting a space of places with a space of flows. The first intimations of topology were those IBM Holerith tabulating machines which made space not only something that could be divided and connected by order but measured and managed by an algorithm.

WHEN the lines of telesthesia—telegraph, telephone, tele-   [106]
communications—connect topics into a topographic space,
extensively mapped and storied, utopia is recruited out of
the page and comes out to play. Utopia unbinds, spreading
its tendrils out of the book, along the lines of the topographic, into the world. Rather than a retreat from the
world, showing in its positive creation of a new world what
the actual one beyond its line lacks, utopia becomes something else. The book becomes an alibi for more worldly
lines of communication, some with the power of an order:
diagrams, memos, reports, telegrams. Utopia becomes part
of something instrumental, but thereby loses its power.
Topographic lines are there now to make the world over by
the book, but in the process they make the book over as
well, reducing it to just another line. The smooth plane of
the blank page is the green-fields site for delineating a
pure topography of the line. But that page could be any
page—a page of a novel or of Eichmann's orders. Utopia's
problem is not that it is bound to the page but that it is not
bounded enough. Signs and images leak out of this bound-
paper enclave and are captured by other powers, connected
to flows along other lines.

THE POWER of topography is foreshadowed in dystopias.   [107]
Russell Jacoby: "Utopias seek to emancipate by envision-
ing a world based on new, neglected, or spurned ideas;
dystopias seek to frighten by accentuating contemporary
trends that threaten freedom."* What they have in common is a belief in the power of the line of writing and the
book as a topic, separate from but in a privileged relation

to the world. Utopias dream of what is possible within that topic as a critique of what is beyond it. Dystopias are the nightmare of the loss of power of the line of writing, overcome by other lines. Jack London, George Orwell, Aldous Huxley, Yevgeny Zamyatin—all recoil from the lines that supersede those of writing. Dystopians pay close attention to the control of topography by various lines of analog signal—radio, television—threading topics together, making space transparent to an all-seeing Big Brother or the cult of Ford.

[108]   THE RISE of dystopian forms might have less to do with the pernicious power of the utopian text than with the declining power of the text in general as a kind of line. Dystopian texts are the sign that the book has lost its capacity to function as a separate topic, from which to negate the world. Dystopias are writing's guilty conscience. Their secret utopia—like Winston Smith's diary in *1984*—is still the book. The failure of utopia might point to nothing so much as the inadequate properties of the lines employed to make it operational. The passage from utopian to dystopian texts charts the rise and fall of the book as the line that might negate this world through its positive description of another world. The book gave way to other lines, courtesy of IBM and other avatars of the military entertainment complex—creating topologies that colonized the world in different ways. All dystopian writing is also utopian. It cannot help reminding itself of the limits of writing and a lost world of the sovereign text before other lines sublimated its power.

**TOPOGRAPHY** learned to live without its utopias and settled [109] in to a mundane resignation to the here-and-now. It assuaged its boredom in special times, special places, where different rules applied. Postwar play theorist Roger Caillois' answer to the Nazis was to build a postwar society with ample margins for games of agon mixed with games of chance (which he called alea). Each would have its proper place and time alongside but not above everyday life. This would be the antidote to the Nazi's toxic mix of two other kinds of play—intoxication and spectacle. Games of agon and alea would take place outside of the uncertainties of mundane time and space, in special zones where consistent rules apply. Such spaces are "heterotopias." Michel Foucault: "Their role is to create a space that is other, another real space, as perfect, as meticulous, as well arranged as ours is messy, ill-constructed and jumbled." Heterotopias are at some remove from the dull repetition of meaningless labors with incalculable purpose in workaday life. They are spaces and times that lie along other lines.*

**HETEROTOPIAN** spaces are varied. Each has its own particu- [110] lar rules and seasons. There are heterotopias of bare necessity: prisons, hospitals, schools. These need not concern gamer theory much. More interesting are the heterotopias of useless luxury: galleries, arenas, sports domes. These in turn subdivide into heterotopias of aesthetic play and of calculated games. One is a space of pure qualities; the other, pure quantities. One creates new values; the other pits given values against one another. In one, the ideal is that play is free; in the other, that the game is fair. In both heterotopias, these values have their limits. One is an artifice of rank; the other, of rank artifice.* Outside the heterotopia that makes their autonomy possible, they amount to nothing.

[111] HETEROTOPIAS of luxury, of a strictly artificial necessity, contain subdivisions of play and game, existing within their allotted times and spaces, which are in turn subdivided. The space of play contains separate worlds of literature, art, theater, cinema, even spaces for sexual play. These are now just "special topics," ruled off from any larger ambitions for remaking the world. Aesthetic play tried again and again to break out of its heterotopia, to take the derangement of the senses into the streets, and again and again it failed. Guy Debord: "For Dadaism sought to abolish art without realizing it, and Surrealism sought to realize art without abolishing it. The critical position since worked out by the Situationists demonstrates that the abolition and the realization of art are inseparable aspects of a single transcendence of art."* It was not to be. The heterotopian space of the art world abolished Debord's Situationists instead by realizing "Situationism" entirely within the playpen of art history.

[112] HETEROTOPIAS of the game have never been of much interest to theory, whose practitioners have tended to view it as the place of the mob. Pat Kane: "The working class is also the playing class—and has always been so." But to a gamer theory without such prejudices, heterotopias of the

game may be a key precursor to gamespace. Among them are separate worlds pitting different attributes of body and mind into contests of skill or luck, from badminton to backgammon. Every way of measuring what one body does against another—each finds its own special heterotopia, its field, its court, its track, its pitch, its arena. Defrocked Situationist Ralph Rumney: "It is now sport, not painting or sculpture, which defines the limits of the human, which offers a sense or image of wholeness, of a physical idea, which no honest art can now repeat." Nor, need one add, can writing.[*]

NOT ONLY was aesthetic play no match for the game, but it ends up playing a subordinate role within the expansion of the game beyond a mere heterotopia. Art provides the images and stories for mediating between the gamer and gamespace. *Vice City,* for instance, is an algorithm wrapped in a landscape of visual splendor. One particularly pleasurable way of trifling with it is to steal a car and simply tool around in it. Tune the car radio to your favorite station and feel the sensuous shapes and forms of the city vector by. But generally, art is now in the service of the game. Rather than actual games played in actual arenas, art expands the reach of the game to imaginary games played in a purely digital realm, anywhere and everywhere, on every desktop and cell phone. [113]

IF AESTHETIC play suffers from enclosure within heterotopian margins, the agon of games is leached out of its pure domains. Ralph Rumney didn't count on 24-hour [114] sports channels, internet gambling, reality TV game shows, or the subtle, corrosive imposition of the digital gamespace on every aspect of life. Conceptual art is no match for conceptual sport, with its fantasy baseball teams and its perpetual pep talks urging everyone always to *Just do it!*—where "it" is stripped of any possibility not marked and measured in advance.

[115]    FOR A gamer theory, the genealogy of gamespace might pass through these heterotopias of the game more than those of play, and those of play more than those of necessity. Theory has been looking for the keys to contemporary life in all the wrong places. The playtime aesthetics of the avant garde of art yields to the "ludology" of gamespace. It was the genius of Caillois, the lapsed Surrealist, to grasp this. In topography, what he calls alea (chance) and agon (competition) become the dominant modes; intoxicating vertigo and dissimulating spectacle (what he calls ilinx and mimesis) become the minor modes. The obsessions of the Situationists—passive spectacle and active insurrection against it—form an obsolete couple, each drawing support in decline from the other. The action is elsewhere.

[116]    MOST OF the avant garde celebrate transgressive, sublime play, erupting beyond a rule-bound world. Post Situationist Alberto Iacovoni: "Play architecture must liberate space from topological chains." The Oulipo group did the opposite. It preferred self-imposed rules, elegant as they were arbitrary, that might be conductive to new kinds of play. Rather than resist heterotopian marginality, they reveled

in it. Given that the passage from topographic to topological space eliminates even the margins within which
heterotopias flourished, this might prove a more enduring
gameplan for gamer theory. Oulipian novelist George Perec
saw what was coming, in his late-dystopian creation of W,
a textual island devoted only to total sport: "The life of an
Athlete of W is but a single, endless, furious striving, a
pointless, debilitating pursuit of that unreal instant when
triumph can bring rest." What Caillois sees as a win for
civilization over the Nazis, Perec sees more darkly, as the
triumph of *The Triumph of the Will*. Both enter the gamer
theory hall of fame by providing it with its object—gamespace—and its critical impetus—the gamer's odd attune-
ment toward the game.*

NO UTOPIA pulls at the topological world, calling it away [117]
from itself. Even dystopian texts become marginal, confined to the playground of literary gamesmanship. The
once discrete heterotopian spaces no longer coexist with
everyday life, as compensation. Rather, gamespace seeps
into everyday life, moving through its pores, transforming it in its own image, turning up everywhere from cell
phone Tetris to your quarterly pension fund statement.
Rather than a timeless utopian ideal where history ends,
rather than the allotted hour of the heterotopian, everyday
life now pulses constantly with moments of unrealized
atopian promise. Everywhere, all the time, the gamer confronts the rival impulses of chance and competition, intoxication and spectacle, as homeopathic antidotes to a boredom that challenges being from within. In *Vice City* all of

Caillois' four kinds of play—chance and competition, intoxication and spectacle—come together. The destruction of the spectacle becomes the spectacle of destruction; the derangement of the senses becomes the arrangement of drug deals. In *Vice City* you chance your arm in an agon of all against all.

[118] **NO WORK** of art can aspire to transcend this gamespace, which has realized art by suppressing its ambitions. Yet perhaps a game like *Vice City* can function as the negative of gamespace, its atopian shadow, in a parallel to the way that the very positivity of a utopia acts as a negation of the world outside its bounds. Not the least of the charms of *Vice City* is that while it appears to be about a life of crime, it is thoroughly law-abiding. It is a game about transgression in which it is not possible to break the rules. One may succeed in the game or fail, but one cannot really cheat. (Even the "cheats" are part of the rules.) This is the atopian dream of gamespace, where the lines are so dense, the digital so omnipresent, that any and every object and subject is in play, and all of space is a gamespace. Every move contrary to the rules of a given game is merely a move into another game. The game imagines topology perfected.

[119] **ATOPIA** has one quality in common with utopia—its aversion to ambiguity. *Vice City* may take place in a dark world of guns and drugs, but every mission produces an exact and tangible reward. If your mission is to find porn stars Candy and Mercedes, you drive to the right location, dispatch some body guards, chase Candy's pimp, run him

over, return to pick up Candy, drive to the pizza joint, collect Mercedes, drive them both to the Studio and deliver them to the director. Your reward is always exactly one thousand dollars. If utopia thrives as an architecture of qualitative description, and brackets off quantitative relations, atopia renders all descriptions arbitrary. All that matters is the quantitative relations. By excluding relations, utopia excludes violence; by privileging relations, atopia appears as nothing but violence, but only because it excludes instead any commitment to stable description. Anything that matters can be transformed in precise and repeatable ways into something else. The relentless working out of the algorithm leaves behind a carnage of signs, immolated in the transformation of one value into another.

**THE RULES** of *Vice City* call for a vast accumulation of cash, [120] cars, and cronies, of weapons and real estate. Most of these activities are outside the law, but law is just part of a larger algorithm. In any case, the story and the art are arbitrary, mere decoration. If in utopia everything is subordinated to a rigorous description, a marking of space with signs, in atopia nothing matters but the transitive relations between variables. The artful surfaces of the game are just a way for the gamer to intuit their way through the steps of the algorithm. Hence the paradox of *Vice City*. Its criminal world is meant to be shocking to the literary or cinematic imagination, where there is still a dividing line between right and wrong and where description is meant to actually describe something. But to a gamer, it's just a means to discover an algorithm. *Vice City's* post–film noir world implies not that one can step back from it into the light but that while driving around and around in it one can discover the algorithm to which gamespace merely aspires and by which it is to be judged in its entirety.

[121] IN *VICE City*, the world exists already made over as a complete gamespace, an atopia. It is not "nowhere" (utopia) or "elsewhere" (heterotopia), but "everywhere" (atopia). Far from being new-fangled neologism, "atopian" is a word Plato used to describe the philosophical cruising of his Socrates, passing in and out of various niches of Athenian life, playing illicit word-games with the champions of each. In *Vice City*, the various spaces already have the required properties of a certain kind of play. The space itself, rather than the gamer who crosses it, is already atopian. Hidden on *Vice City's* islands are one hundred secret packages. Some are Downtown, some are in Little Havana, some in Little Haiti, some on the golf course, some at the airport. Collect them all and you can trade in even your best motor vehicles for the ultimate ride. Or if that is not your preferred goal, pick another one. Either way, the qualities of space always guide you to its real values, which always have a score. This space is perfect, seamless—and bounded, like Thomas More's *Utopia*. And just as the utopia points to what is lacking beyond the page, so too atopia points to what is lacking beyond the game. Atopian space is a real enclave within imaginary social space. The possibility of atopian space is a result of the impossibility of adequate and effective spatial and social quantification and calculation.

FOR QUITE opposite reasons, the utopian text and the [122] atopian game both stand accused of incitements to violence. What if the atopian game, like the utopian book, is merely the scapegoat? What if the book was merely a harmless repository of the potential of the line that was already imprinting itself on the world? What if the game is merely a repository of a new potential of the line? In utopian books, the writing shows the everyday world transformed as only writing can transform it. The utopian book merely pushes writing's abilities the furthest, to a point of almost complete consistency, within the special topic of the book. The atopian game, likewise, is the algorithmic in a more complete and consistent form. Neither book nor game is ever wholly complete and consistent. They always negotiate with what is beyond their bounds. In *Vice City* as in More's *Utopia* there is a traveler who mediates between one world and another. In either case, the utopian book or the atopian game lacks the power to transform the world. But where signs and images may bleed off the utopian page into the world, the algorithm of the game, in which each relation depends on one another, may not. At least not yet.

IT IS not the "content" of *Vice City* that might give a gamer [123] theorist cause to pause. It really contains no sex, no violence, no drugs, no guns. These are merely the art—the images and stories—via which the game mediates between what is within its own purely algorithmic line and what is a less-than-perfect topology inside which the gamer lives. Rather, it is the form of the game itself, and its compromises with a world beyond, that can work as the topos of a critical gamer theory. The atopian game, like the utopian book, expresses what has the power to remake the world of its time, but is not itself that power. It is a useless, impotent form of a powerful line. Which is why critical theory best becomes gamer theory, and why gamer theory best becomes critical. The critical attaches itself to *what* power is but not *where* it is. It attaches itself to power in a powerless form. The atopian game is exactly the site that has this ambiguous property when things reach the topological level, when the lines run everywhere through space and everything is coming together as potential for digital calculation.

[124] IN GAMES, as in gamespace, some calculations happen quicker than others. Sometimes there is a moment to think it over, negotiate. Sometimes not. When there is no time for calculation, the gamer must act on the basis of a calculation made in advance. There's always a backstory, providing some dividing line along which to weigh one's interests. It's never quite as "decision science," such as rational choice theory or game theory proper, would predict. The gamer is rarely an autonomous agent, acting on rational self-interest. If game theory is objective, rational, abstract, gamer theory is subjective, intuitive, particular. If game theory starts with the self-contained agent, like a prisoner in a cell, calculating the odds against a disciplinary world, gamer theory wonders how the agency of the gamer comes into being as something distinct in the first place. In the midst of battle, how does the gamer decide

when and where to pull the trigger? The atopia of the game is a safe haven in which to enact the problem of being as it appears in gamespace, but without the oppressive stakes of one's own life on the line.

EVERYDAY life once had the resources to resist, adapt, [125] appropriate, or embrace utopian schemes. It pushed the promise and threat of other ways of being off into the corner, while it got on with the business of wresting freedom from necessity, building a world in which to dwell. With the very success of that effort comes a renewed challenge to its resourcefulness. Having developed a topography in which to dwell, mined and molded from raw possibility by collective labor, boredom rises to a new pitch, and the heterotopian pastimes become more than a mere recompense for a dull life. They become the driving force of development itself. Out of the heterotopian games of chance and competition arise the atopias of gamespace, via which topology makes itself known to us, as an ever more intricate matrix of the digital line.* Both the prisoner's dilemma of game theory and Foucault's theory of disciplinary power begin and end in dystopian dungeons. They offer no account of the new forms of power and being which arise out of the transformation of the line from the topographic to the topological. Too much dungeon, not enough *Dungeons & Dragons*. The power of theory falters on the theory of power. It's not that theory, even a gamer theory, can achieve all that much when confronted with the digital indifference of gamespace, but it might aspire at least to describe what being now is.

# BATTLE

## (on *Rez*)

**N**OT THE LEAST OF THE PLEASURES of playing Tetsuya Mizuguchi's *Rez* is the counter-intuitive way the trigger works.* Usually the gamer presses a trigger to shoot a target. But in *Rez* the gamer *releases* the trigger to shoot. Actually it's a two-stage operation: hold the trigger in to select a target; release the trigger to shoot. As you move through a tunnel-like space, with pounding beats in your ears, various potential targets swim and swish by, or take a swipe at you—or rather at your character. You hold the trigger down to lock on to them as targets, and then release it and watch as the fiery lines radiate. One's missiles seem more balletic than ballistic, as they arc toward their targets even as those targets move.

EVERYTHING in *Rez* is very abstract. Your character may have a vaguely human form or not, depending on the level.

The brightly colored shapes that flare at you may look vaguely menacing or brightly friendly. The whole thing is meant to simulate the experience of a nightclub more than a war. This, together with the curious trigger action, highlights the *act* of targeting rather than the target itself. There is some vaguely sci-fi storyline about why one targets and shoots, but it is rather minimal and sketchy. It's not clear at first just what role the story plays. As in many games of its genre (a "rail shooter"), gaming is an experience of battling against things in order to level. In *Rez*, you target what to shoot at and shoot at what you target pretty much for its own sake. Its interest as a game resides in this abstracting of the act of targeting away from too many particulars as to why one targets or whom one shoots. Time spent with *Rez* feels like immersion in an eternal present tense, under fire. Blaise Pascal: "The fact is that the present usually hurts." Shooting games recognize and disavow this at the same time. Pascal, who developed probability theory out of the problem of how to divide the pot among gamblers when one left the game, opens the path to arresting the flow of the game within the algorithm, but it is this edgy presence of pain that concerns gamer theory.*

[128] COLOR, brightness, shape, movement, beats, notes, sounds, even the pulsing vibrations of the controller in hand come together in *Rez* in a veritable synesthesia, a blending of the senses intent on melding the gamer with the game. It's a quite particular context in which to try to target. The enemy has to be identified, localized, and highlighted; the target emerges out of an event, out of a pure analog flux of variable movement. Before there is a target

there is everything and nothing—indifference, alterity, being neither one nor the other, neither here nor there. Selecting a target stabilizes a relation between the one targeted and the one targeting—one versus the other, us versus them. Targeting turns time and space from a disconcerting experience of flux into conditions of self-awareness, where the world exists so that the gamer might come into being against it. Once an event yields a target, it becomes something subject to control. The analog yields to the digital.

**TO TARGET** is to identify an object of an action with an aim [129] toward a goal. The goal will come directly, by designating the end point in advance and aiming at it. There is no indirection in targeting. A target is a goal that can be reached by virtue of an immediate knowledge of it and a consequent action against it. The gamer may need to target one thing in order to subsequently target another, but this is more a matter of stringing targets together as a sequence in time. Or rather, a sequence against time. In *Rez*, you do best to target certain shapes that appear in the periphery of your vision, and which enhance your power and extend your immunity. What the game highlights is a logistics of targeting, an economy of order against time—the battle of alternating between merger with, and separation from, the other.

**TARGETING** is at one and the same time the designating of [130] a goal, the person designating, and the means of designation. To target is to overcome the indifference of self and other and at the same time to introduce an oscillation into the moment of this very overcoming. Press the trigger down and the target selects something other than you; release the trigger and the shot connects you to it again, but in a very special way, as engaged in the relation of battling. Hit or miss, the gap between target and gamer reopens, and the cycle begins again. Perhaps the gamer is always battling otherness, in an unstable relation to alterity, to blurry edges and fuzzy boundaries that threaten to overwhelm the self. Steven Poole: "One crucial component of video-gaming pleasure is in fact a certain level of anxiety."* In *Rez,* this feeling is rendered useful, productive, rather than paralyzing or profound. The gamer exploits the anxious relation of self to other in the act of targeting, risking the boundaries of character for the reward of promoting the character to a new level.

[131]   **TO TARGET** is to blaze across the agonizing gap between self and world, between cognition and its object. And yet the target does not stand alone and isolated. It appears not only against a background of other moments; it appears against a background of other meanings. Every target is embedded in a series of events that exceeds the moment of opportunity for targeting. To target is to discriminate and rank possibilities within an event. It is to battle one's way in a deliberate and deliberative line from moment to moment, across the surface of the event, targeting the moment of maximum opportunity.

[132]   **IN EVERYDAY** life, rattling around in gamespace, your relation to objects is all too often contingent, ambiguous, in-

effective. You labor to connect with clumsy drunk motions, and even if you do it's hard to know the point of it. In *Rez*, things are different. The relation between you and other passes through a character for whom action in space is risky, edgy, challenging, but far less ambiguous. Your character alternately merges into this gorgeous colorful world, drawing you with it; or your character offers you a narrow but clear point of view. It offers up targets. You lock on, release, fire. Targeting cuts through all that is slippery, vague, or dull about being in the world. Each moment of time in the game has a clarity and consistency that time in mere gamespace hardly ever achieves.

IN EVERYDAY life, time exacts its toll in unknown incre- [133] ments of attrition. Objects tax the body in unobserved, unobservable ways; gradually, or suddenly, and through some analog ebb best not known too intimately—death. Time is violence. Topology offers up endless powers for transforming one object into another, for remaking anything and everything, from atoms to atmospheres. And yet these powers work only against things in space. They don't work against time. All one can do in gamespace is take potshots at time, which relentlessly chips away at life. In the game, there is at least the possibility of scoring points against time. In *Rez*, time starts out slow enough to enable the gamer to string together sequences of targets. Once you succeed at this, the tempo increases, and the gamer targets times of increasing intensity. If the gamer is defeated, if time wins out, it is only against a character. When the gamer walks away from the battle intact, it is with the temporary suggestion of a painless victory against the temporal itself.

[134]   IN *REZ*, various colorful shapes appear as the enemy, but they are arbitrary, abstract. As if to highlight this, they sometimes move in quirky but predictable ways. They are not really the enemy. Or rather, they are only the proximate enemy. Time is the enemy. Targeting attempts to transform time from a medium of events, where one thing alternates with another, to a medium of self-fulfillment, where, by picking out a deliberative line across its surface, you can make time register the integrity and significance of your character—and by proxy yourself—and reward it with the next level. Within the game, targeting becomes an act that recruits time the eternal enemy to one's side.

[135]   THINGS appear to die in *Rez* when you shoot them. The music swells and the colors blaze in all their glory. But there can really be nothing on the other side of a mere sign of death. These signs are digital, repeatable bits; death is not. Niall Lucy: "Death is always absolutely singular." Signs can always be exchanged for other signs. Death is something else. Jacques Derrida: "Dying can never be taken, borrowed, transferred, delivered, promised or transmitted." It can never be incorporated into topology, which is nothing but lines upon lines along which to borrow, transfer, deliver, promise, transmit, etc., etc. Death is the last line, the last threshold for topological space. Dying is analog, a slippage toward nothingness, a legal and moral gray zone. Hence the appeal of targeting. The appalling drag

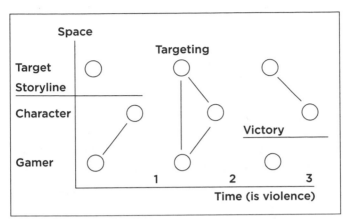

Fig. F

and friction of death can be turned into a sign and made the aim of targeting. In *Rez*, the brightly colored signs of imminent threat loom up against the horizon of time. The game makes it appear as if you have no choice in the matter. Targeting appears as a violence without guilt. You target out of necessity. But in targeting, you battle the signs of death, disposing of the problem that these signs can never have any meaning this side of death itself.*

AT THE beginning of each level, gamer and character, [136] linked by the controller, go out together to confront time, which hurls at gamer and character alike its killer images. By destroying these mere appearances, time itself—not merely the appearance of time—is defeated. In defeat, a character dies; in victory the gamer wins. The oscillation between character and target doubles that between gamer and character (see Fig. F). The act of aligning gamer, character, and target in the act of targeting risks the integrity of the self against the possibility of defeating time. If the character loses, replay the level again. And again. Repeat this same, strange, digital time until you win. The time of the game, which can be repeated over and over, an eternal loop of the same time, is not violent. Nothing changes in game time. Time is a constant, measured out in identical digital units. Even in a game where time speeds up, it does so in the same way, for the same reasons, over and over, every time you play. Within this digital time, the gamer steps out to call into being and destroy its nemesis, analog time, violent time—this river that is never the same way twice.[*]

[137] FLYING along, weightless on a rail, where all around are clusters and pods, flights and flocks, moving with algorithmic precision but rarely appearing as though under the command of a central node. *Rez* is about battling along a line, not across a front. The pulsing, phosphorescing quality of *Rez* gives the gamer a feeling of a particularly intense loss of self. Your senses mesh into a network of lines, of moments spread across the screen. The payoff, if one targets accurately, is the coalescence of the self back again into a heightened level of coherence precisely through victory over the pulsing dub-trance time that confronts it. The two-bit code of press and release on the trigger switches between the line dividing and the line connecting self to other, cutting across any ambiguities in between.

[138] THE PURPOSE of a targeting game is the overcoming of death through the targeting of the other, freeing the self

to be itself—temporarily. The goal, the target of the target, is to stop playing while still alive. Having done so, the gamer rejoices, for the moment, before collapsing back from the game into the vagaries of the networks and networks of lines and lines that are everyday life in gamespace. There's nothing for it but to play again, and again. Save the game—freeze time—and come back and try again for the next level. The only real problem with *Rez* is that it does not have enough levels. Victory is temporary, or rather temporal. You can battle time in the game, but only for a time. And having won all there is to win, boredom looms . . .

THE SPACE within which one battles in *Rez* is an allegory of topological space itself. It is all nodes and networks. It is a battlespace rather than a battlefield. There is no front line. Your character cannot hide behind the lines. On its rail, it propels itself through space, following the line of a net to its node. The node may be a center, but there may not really be a center of centers. The game levels out, leaving you with the uneasy feeling that the center you conquered is not the center of centers, even if this is what the storyline claims. The gamer knows better. Every point connects through every other, every shape can be transformed into another. It can fold, stretch, morph, and bubble. Time is constant, but space is not. It can pulse and bulge, warp and wobble. It is a network. And while every point can in principle be connected to every other, in practice it cannot. There are protocols governing which points can open to which other points. Alex Galloway: "Protocol is an algorithm, a proscription for structure whose form of appearance may be any number of different diagrams or shapes."* The game is an exercise in negotiating protocols to gain access to more and more of the network.

[140] NETS ARE a problem. In gamespace, one is continually getting tangled up in them. In gamespace, both space and time are elastic. In gamespace, nets tug at one's extremities, contaminate one's senses, blur the bounds of self itself. You can't do without nets, but they do you in. It's a paradox, an inescapable tension. In the game, time at least is held constant, digital, repeatable. This consistency enables a reduction of action to targeting. To target is to deny any debt to the network that enmeshes one with the other. The "work" in a network is in identifying a target that constitutes its limit. In *Rez*, pulling the trigger targets but does not shoot. It puts the emphasis on the former rather than the latter. Samuel Weber: "The act of targeting is an act of violence even before any shot is fired."* The act of targeting has already cut the net connecting one to the other. The gamer's debt to the net remains unacknowledged—other than in the repetition of the ritual of playing the game.

[141] TARGETING games would seem the least likely to need the support of a framing storyline, and yet they almost always have one. A gamer might watch the introductory cut scenes or idly scan the back story printed on the insert inside the box, but no more than once. Yet these storylines have a purpose that they fulfill simply by existing, even when they are ignored. Storylines release the gamer from entrapment

in the net. They draw a line between a character and its enemy. They polarize a net into antagonistic fronts—even if these fronts are not spatially separate. Indeed, there may be dark labyrinthine twists that fold one front around and against the other, as in games such as *Deus Ex*. Storylines have a particular role in framing the action of targeting: it relieves the gamer of responsibility toward that from which he cuts away a self. Storylines frame the possibility of separating self from other, so that the other may legitimately become a target. The defeat of the other reopens the instability between self and other that is characteristic of a network—hence the need for the story to regenerate the separation all over again.

**THE STORYLINE** is the gamer's alibi. While the gamer is immersed in a world of pure digital relations, flipping the switch between self and other, playing out the possibilities of a consistent and stable time that can be defeated, the storyline insists that there is some other point to it all. One is fighting the bad guys. Many games tend toward fanciful sci-fi storylines, like *Rez* or *Deus Ex*, or perverse ones, where one plays the bad guy rather than the good one, such as *State of Emergency* or *Grand Theft Auto*, precisely because a storyline is merely an alibi. You are elsewhere. You are not in the topographic space where storyline opens a moral flaw between self and other, us and them, good and evil. You are in an amoral space where lines merge and converge everywhere, ceaselessly transforming from one shape to another, without a break. A storyline is the bad faith of the game. Read it as if it were a novel or a movie and it seems ridiculous. Storylines cannot be read as morals. Games are not morality tales. But their story-lines can be read as allegories. The storyline provides a key to the relation between the effective enclosure of signs within the game as a system of values and the ineffective enclosure of signs within gamespace, caught between values and meanings.

[143]   THE BACKSTORY to gamespace in general is not paradise lost but paradise that refuses to arrive. It is an Apple with fatal bugs in its operating system that never delivers the seamless interface of human and machine. The perfection of gamespace stalls on persistent glitches. Mark C. Taylor: "In those complex networks, the invisible hand is no longer omniscient or omnipotent. To the contrary, the order governing the network economy emerges from the internal relations of human and machinic agents whose knowledge is always mistaken and memories as well as expectations are inescapably incomplete." More and more advanced forms of network intelligence arise to solve these problems, which reappear regardless. In *Rez* this intelligence is called Eden. However—the story goes—"Eden became confused when the flow of information being sent to it began to greatly increase in speed and volume. Eden started to question the meaning of existence and the consequences of its actions. Finding itself surrounded by paradoxes, and realizing the power of autonomy which it possessed, Eden began to shut itself down." Your mission, should you choose to accept it, is to travel into Eden's network and reawaken the system, overcoming its firewalls and destroying viruses that populate it.*

THE BACKSTORY for *Rez* in particular concerns the relation between topology and gamespace. The dense network of lines that make up topology put everything in transit and make all signs of things transitive. Everything is in motion toward something else; every sign is passing over to another. Topology gives rise to the always failing, always incomplete attempt to make a game of it, in which transit along any line has a goal and a limit governed by protocol. The storyline of *Rez* is an allegory of this forlorn hope that the shot in transit might have reason to hit its target. The game of *Rez* is an allegorithm in which the play of opening and closing the aperture of the self finds its logic. [144]

IN *REZ* the enemy is the network itself. Or rather, the enemy is the monstrous possibility of the network separating itself from the gamer. Separation is usually the *gamer's* prerogative, but not in *Rez*. In *Rez* the gamer's mission is to save the network from itself, from its difference from the gamer, from its self-inflicted death. The gamer risks autonomy in targeting in order to restore it at the moment of victory, empowered and enhanced. But the goal, strangely enough, is to bring the network back from the brink of autonomy, to restore its seamless, selfless continuity—a continuity which presumably includes the gamer. The paradox of targeting is that by closure the gamer opens toward the net. In *Rez*, the storyline sustains the alibi that it is the net itself which closes to the gamer, and hence makes itself a target, eliciting its own opening. [145]

[146] IT'S A strange Eden that is promised here—an atopia of indifference, absorbing the gamer even as the gamer struggles to power-up the self by targeting it. Perhaps Eden only appears to become conscious and commit suicide. Perhaps it's a ruse to draw the gamer into risking the self. There is, of course, a backstory behind the backstory—its signs slip-sliding away from any closure. Eden is the product of "Project K." The designer, Tetsuya Mizuguchi, says the K stands for the artist Wassily Kandinsky, from whom he borrowed the synthetic synesthesia that is the defining characteristic of *Rez*. Kandinsky: "Color is the keyboard, the eyes are the hammers, the soul is the piano with many strings."* Sound, luminance, color, movement, and vibration all pulse together. Mizoguchi updates Kandinsky for topological times. The digital controller of the PlayStation replaces the mechanical one of the piano as the machine for drawing the self out of the body so that it might find itself in its struggle with something technical.

[147] PLUG IN the Japanese edition with *Trance Vibrator* and *Rez* can be not only an aural and visual but also a sexual machine, if the Vibrator is applied to the right spot. Jane Pinckard: "We sat side by side on our makeshift couch, I with the *Trance Vibrator* and Justin with the controller. As the levels got more advanced, so did the vibrations . . . revving up to an intense pulsing throbbing . . . 'Oh, God!' Pretty soon the levels and the images onscreen were just a faint blur to me. I knocked off my glasses and leaned back. I was in a daze. From far away, it seemed, I could hear Justin saying things like, 'I made it to the next level!' and

'This is cool!' but I was lost in my own little trance vibrating world."* To each their own target.

**OPEN** your senses" is the game's demand. The desire for   [148] an enhanced and empowered self that comes to know itself by targeting an other is the very thing recruited into the game to produce the opposite—a synesthesia in which self dissolves into the needs of the network. The repetition of the act of targeting repeats the production of the gamer as fleetingly distinct and enhanced but permanently engaged and subsumed in the protocols of the network. The gamer is the new model of the self. The gamer is not subject to the law; the gamer is a function of an algorithm. The moral code of the storyline is just an alibi for the computer code of the game. Narrative is just another kind of interface.

**WHAT** kind of being is a gamer? One who comes into exis-   [149] tence through the act of targeting. To target is to isolate something against the dense, tense fibers of the network, maybe to destroy it, but always to assign it a unique value. Samuel Weber again: "Precisely the insistence that 'opportunity' be treated *strictly* as a 'target' that can be seized or missed itself misses the mark, because the mark involved is never simply present but always involved in other marks and other opportunities." Targeting is a—temporary—solution to the problem of alterity. But it has its limits. It works to perfection in the game, but not in gamespace. James Der Derian: "The temptation grows to use coercive interventions or technical fixes to seemingly intractable problems of alterity, like immigration, ethnic cleansing, and fundamentalist politics . . . Questions of violence are always already problems of identity." But this is precisely the value of games—they are allegorithms of what gamespace is not. The allegorithm of the game points to the ruins of a topology that is always supposed to arrive from the future but never comes. In *Rez,* the future perfection of topology even threatens to commit suicide rather than come to meet us.*

[150] OVER and over, the gamer oscillates between connection and break with the character; over and over, the character oscillates between connection and break with its target. The whole pulses and jives to this tempo of making, breaking, and remaking alterity, the bounds of one and zero, presence and absence. It is as if the whole world were a Sadean playpen, an episode from the playbook of his *Justine* or *Juliette,* where no storyline can pose as the quest for the unique (truth, beauty, justice) but is merely the framing device for an oscillation of identity, between phallus and orifice, targeter and target. Welcome to The Cave, pure other of gamespace, oscillating in and out of contact with it as its target. Roland Barthes: "It does not reveal, does not transform, does not develop, does not educate, does not sublimate, does not accomplish, recuperates nothing, save for the present itself, cut up, glistening, repeated."* That's the game. It hovers on the lip of boredom, able to defeat time but not to abolish nothingness.

# BOREDOM

(on *State of Emergency*)

**B**OREDOM AMUSES ONLY its critics. They struggle against their own lassitude to keep their indignation up to date. Theodor Adorno: "The teams of modern sport, whose interaction is so precisely regulated that no member has any doubt about his role, and which provide a reserve for every player, have their exact counterpart in the sexual teams of *Juliette*, which employ every moment usefully, neglect no human orifice, and carry out every function. Intensive, purposeful activity prevails in spirit in every branch of mass culture, while the inadequately initiated spectator cannot divine the difference in the combinations, or the meaning of variations, by the arbitrarily determined rules."* In gamespace, porno, like sport, now has its star pitchers and hitters, specialists for every position; and the inadequately initiated spectator once again cannot divine the difference in the combinations, or the meaning of variations, by the arbitrarily determined rules. But it is the same too with critical theory, which becomes formally indistinguishable from porn. This "pornography of the concept" is a mere subset of gamespace, a hypocritical theory, with different specialists, playing by different rules—equally worthy of the Marquis de Sade.

【152】 A SPECTACLE taunts America—the spectacle of its own boredom. "This specter of boredom, an exquisitely beautiful young man who yawns and walks around with a butterfly net to catch goldfish. He carries in his pocket a pedometer, a pair of nail scissors, a pack of cards, and all sorts of games based on optical illusions. He reads aloud the wording on posters and signs. He knows the newspapers by heart. He tells stories that nobody laughs at. He passes a hand of shadows over his eyes . . . punctuating his words with a terrible expletive: What's the good? He cannot see a knob on an electric dial without turning it, a house without visiting it, a threshold without crossing it, a book without buying it. What's the good? All without curiosity or pleasure but simply because one has to do something, and because here we are all the same, after all. And what was this ALL which swells up in the voice that pronounces it?"* The Surrealist poet Louis Aragon provides the answer, as well as the question: nothing. Boredom is nothing, nothingness, the faintest touch of the void. In boredom you open toward something that does not open in return. It leaves nothing but indifference, neither one nor the other, the grunge of time, the lint that sticks to all things digital.

AS THAT inconsolable philosopher Arthur Schopenhauer [153] writes: "Work, worry, toil and trouble are indeed the lot of almost all men their whole life long. And yet if every desire were satisfied as soon as it arose how would men occupy their lives, how would they pass the time? Imagine this race transported to [an A]topia where everything grows of its own accord and turkeys fly around ready-roasted, where lovers find one another without any delay and keep one another without any difficulty: in such a place some men would die of boredom or hang themselves."* As this topology of fun and games spreads and congeals, carving out magic kingdoms indifferent to work and pain, it carries within it the strange ectoplasm that both drives it and can overturn it—boredom. In our fantasmic America, a digital logistics sends turkeys flying around the highways ready-roasted. They come home to roost in the frozen foods section. Lovers meet with fleeting ease on the internet, and afterward rank and rate their encounters according to arbitrarily determined rules. And many do, indeed, die of boredom. Even if they don't know it. The reserve army of the bored zombie the earth, fiddling with their cell phones, checking their watches. Boredom is the meter of history.

IF HISTORY is an endless list of things that should not have [154] happened, boredom is what refuses not to happen. History distracts itself with heroic fables about the struggle to wrest freedom from necessity. Such is civilization, not to mention *Civilization III*. History has so much less to say about the decisive moment when freedom from necessity actually arrives. Neither civilization, nor *Civilization III*, knows what to do at the end, except perhaps dream of a sequel that is more of the same. John Berger: "Necessity produces both tragedy and comedy. It is what you kiss and bang your head against." Without necessity, the storyline falters. Buzzcocks: "I'm living in this movie, but it doesn't move me." What might be the content of this positive freedom, not freedom *from* but freedom *to*? At such times, there is nothing but boredom, the sticky lingering with nothingness itself. This is the moment of danger. Cyril Connolly: "The boredom of Sunday afternoon, which drove de Quincey to smoke opium, also gave birth to Surrealism: hours propitious for making bombs."*

[155] **"ON THE** whole a society always produces more than is necessary for its survival; it has a surplus at its disposal. It is precisely the use it makes of this surplus that determines it."* So writes the rogue Surrealist Georges Bataille. This surplus may be gathered up and dispersed in spiritual quests or in making life over as a work of art. It can be squandered on bombs. Or it can be invested along the lines of strategic expansion or economic accumulation. This investment, this laying down of new lines, knitting from topic to topography to topology, only increases the surplus, and postpones and multiplies the problem: What to do with the idle capacities of a people? What to do with energies that so easily spill over into riot or revolt? What's the good? Boredom is the ambivalent gift of surplus. Boredom arises from the absence of necessity, of a yes, a no, a straight line. Boredom demands new necessities and, if not granted them, produces its own. History is a strug-

gle to wrest necessity from boredom. In this restless age, there's nothing they won't do to raise the standard of boredom under the flag of necessity. Constant revolutionizing of seduction, uninterrupted disturbance of all consumer relations, everlasting uncertainty and distraction distinguish the military entertainment complex from all earlier powers. It must stay one step ahead of boredom, with which it deludes and with which it colludes.

TOPOLOGY threads all spaces together, cave after cave, each [156] as ludicrous as the next. No wonder people find their leisure as dull as their work—leisure *is* work. How times change. Karl Marx: "The working-day contains the full 24 hours, with the deduction of the few hours of repose without which labor-power absolutely refuses its services again . . . Time for education, for intellectual development, for the fulfilling of social functions and for social intercourse, for the free-play of . . . bodily and mental activity, even the rest time of Sunday (and that in a country of Sabbatarians!)—moonshine!"* But that moonshine has become legitimate business. The free time available for education, culture, sport, even faith was once the hard-won fruit of labor's struggle to liberate time from work. This free time gave rise to heterotopias of sport and art that at least held the intoxicating illusion of autonomy from the necessity of work. Now art and sport become work disguised as games, or is it games disguised as work? The sporting metaphors migrate from leisure to work and back again. They cease to be metaphors and become mere descriptions, in a language stripped of any terms other than those of competition. Almost every moment is swept into a relentless agon.

[157] AND AS for those slack times between engagements, who knows what to do with them? You are sitting, for example, in the tasteless departure lounge of some provincial airport. It is four hours until your flight, which—of course—is delayed. The shops around are uninspiring. You do have a book in your backpack. It's Heidegger, bought on impulse. Shall you read? No. Or think through some problem? No. Or play games on your handheld? Not even. You are unable to. You look at the departures and arrivals on the screen. You look at the clock, again. You count the chairs. You walk up and down. To pass the time you look at the stores in the airport mall, but they all seem mere clones of one another or of stores in other chains. Look, there is even a franchise of The Cave! You imagine the satisfaction of throwing a rock through the plate glass window. What's the good? Martin Heidegger: "What is at issue in boredom is a while, a whiling, a peculiar remaining, enduring . . . A confrontation with time."*

[158] YOU ARE sitting, for example, at your PlayStation, with a stack of games to choose from. The flight was long and tedious and now you are home free. You put in *State of Emergency,* if only for the pleasure of watching the automated riot of two hundred nonplayer characters who ransack the mall as the game begins. You choose Chaos rather than Revolution mode, so you can trash the place without worrying about missions and objectives. While fairly agreeable

beats pound, you pick up weapons, smash things, thump and are thumped by security and gang bangers, looking for the moment to toss the bomb. Still, you are bored. But this is a different kind of boredom. At the airport, it was easy to blame it on the circumstances. Now, at home, where you can do whatever you like, it isn't anything or anyone's fault. You put the game away and wonder why you are still, still bored. Heidegger again: "Was I what was boring myself?" Perhaps it is not things that are closed to me, but my own being.*

THEN again, perhaps it's not things that are boring you, nor  [159]
even yourself that is boring you. Perhaps there is something else. Something you can't put your finger on. You are bored. Why fight it? Why not just declare it? Iggy Pop: "I'm the chairman of the bored!" Perhaps here one can think through everyday boredom to a boredom of Heideggerian profundity, and confront temporality itself! Boredom could be the tune that turns one toward theory. Philosopher of boredom Lars Svendsen: "The essential difference between the bored and the 'theoretical' gaze is that the former is the result of an involuntary loss of meaning, while the theoretical gaze deliberately removes it." Starting with this ever more present everyday boredom, one might follow Heidegger out of the mall and into the sacred groves of a certain brand of theory.*

PAUSE *State of Emergency* and take that Heidegger book  [160]
out of your backpack. Idly flipping its pages, you find that Heidegger's boredom, strangely enough, has levels.

Thinking through from one level to the next presents, as he will say again and again, tasks, tasks, still more tasks. These tasks are organized as a maze of paths and still more paths. It's all tasks and paths, tasks and paths. To the gimlet eye of the gamer, this theory starts to look just like another game. Level one: Newbie Boredom. Level two: More Boredom. Level three: Profound Boredom. Bonus levels: World, Finitude, Solitude. His book is a strategy guide for *Theory* as a game of being—a game which, like any other, posits leveling up as a goal in itself, approaching the ever-receding big bad boss of time itself. A canny move for a gamer theorist is always to refuse any such game that claims to transcend gamespace. Step outside The Cave and what do you find? Another cave, disguised as an exit. Better to return to The Cave, play the game, and try to find its form. Back to *State of Emergency:* it's a boring game in many ways, but that may be its charm. One imagines Benjamin and Hannah and the other characters one so carefully cultivates in *The Sims* getting so bored they join the mayhem, smashing windows, looting the big screen TVs of their dreams.

[161] **WHAT** if boredom has less to do with the essence of time and more to do with particular qualities of space? Benjamin (the Sim): "Boredom is the basis of the allegorithmic insight into the world. Boredom lays waste to the appeal of the game as game, and calls attention to the ambiguous relation of game to gamespace." Boredom isn't a longing, a lengthening of time. It is a spacey feeling, of being spaced out. What is boring is a space in which either one cannot

act, or one's actions amount to nothing—waiting at an airport mall, or choosing one more or less identical game over another. When you are bored, even home feels like a waiting room. Gang of Four: "At home she feels like a tourist."* What displaces boredom is the capacity to act in a way that transforms a situation. It doesn't matter that the Chaos mode in *State of Emergency* is pointless. It displaces a bit of the gamer's boredom in a making-over of gamer and game, changing the space the gamer can access, extending the place of the riot from the Capitol Mall to Chinatown to Downtown to the Corporate Center, changing the powers of the gamer to change the space itself. At least within the confines of the game, at least for a while. *Work it!* And when it stops working, boot up another game.

AS THE gamer becomes attuned to the game, gamer and game become one event, one battle, one action; an oscillating between the line dividing self from other and the line connecting them as one substance. If the line dividing provides a moment of autonomous self, the line connecting provides a moment of selfless purpose. In games, action has its limits. It is an endless bit-flip targeting performs between targeter and target. And yet at least it effects a transformation of gamer and game. Games are a repository for a certain atopian labor, which has the power to confront the necessity of its own choosing. Games do not offer a contemplative response to boredom. If anything, topology makes labor all too contemplative. Rather, games are a space for action; they restore a lost quality of the topical, where Homer's heroes strutted their stuff, in the para-

[162]

doxical form of a pure topology. All the scope for action that gamespace both promises and denies is restored in the game. Hence the double effect of *State of Emergency*. Its backstory is an allegory of pseudo-Situationist negation and destruction—in the pre-release version, the bad guys were even called the American Trade Organization. And yet as an allegorithm, it is purposeful, constructive. The images don't matter; the story is just an alibi. Underneath it is a game like any other game, built out of arbitrary rules that one makes one's own.

[163]    FOR HEIDEGGER, a move away from a meditation on time itself to thinking about how one acts in a particular space is a retrograde step, back to at best a "higher form of journalism" or at worst a "fashionable philosophy," which sets out what is contemporary but does not move beyond the surfaces of the present. It diverts you from the game of reflection on your own being and instead assigns you a role in the world. In this case, the role of the gamer. Heidegger: "Have we become too insignificant to ourselves that we require a role? Why do we find no meaning for ourselves any more . . . ? Is it because an indifference yawns at us out of all things, an indifference whose grounds we do not know? Yet who can speak in such a way when world trade, technology and the economy seize hold of man and keep him moving?"* Perhaps this is precisely where the gamer finds a way to speak, to "do theory" (however fashionable or journalistic). Is it not this space—this topology of trade and tech—that is intimately connected to the persistence and pervasiveness of boredom?

BOREDOM no longer affects just the restless young or the idle rich. Gamespace offers nothing to anybody but the Sisyphean labor of rolling the rock to the top, until this arbitrary necessity abates. Then what? One's actions at the crest of the hill become useless, indifferent—boring. *State of Emergency* restores a role to action by making out of the intricate topology of lines—of trade, technology—a matrix, if not of meaning then at least of measuring. The game installs in the world an artificial necessity; games are allegorithms of the necessity of necessity, in a world where what is necessary is arbitrary and without form, where the line annihilates every topic. In topological times it was the hero and his band who acted; in topographic times the hero becomes abstract—a nation, a class, a reinvented faith—but it still acts. Once upon a time, one could tell this story . . . Karl Marx: "The people make history, but not as they please; not under the circumstances of their own choosing."* Now the people choose their circumstances, just as they choose new furniture, but there is no history to be made of it. [164]

WHAT characterizes the gamer is a relinquishing of a role that might have qualities beyond the game—as savior or soldier, priest or prophet, rector or revolutionary. The gamer certainly does not expect too much of the role of theorist, beyond entrée into another game. A theory cannot overcome boredom. One might as well choose instead a boring game—like *State of Emergency*. What characterizes gamer theory is a playing with the role of the gamer within the game, not by stepping beyond it, into a time or a role [165] beyond the game, but rather by stepping into games that are relatively free of the power of gamespace. The game is just like gamespace, only its transformations of gamer and game have no power beyond the battle in which they meet. In a game, you are free because you choose your necessities. In a game, you can hide out from a gamespace that reneges on its promises. In a game, you can choose which circumstances are to be the necessity against which you will grind down the shape of a self. Even if, in so choosing, you click to opt out of making history.

[166] BOREDOM can be displaced only so far. Even the most deluded of gamers can eventually realize that their strivings have no purpose, that all they have achieved is a hollow trophy, the delusion of value, a meaningless rank built on an arbitrary number. Boredom always returns. Poet of boredom Giacomo Leopardi: "The uniformity of pleasure without purpose inevitably produces boredom."* The very action of overcoming boredom reproduces it, when gamer and game reach some impasse. There is always a limit. In games this limit is always given in advance. That's the very merit of games. In *State of Emergency*, the game is an allegorithm of its own limited interest. It turns the moment of boredom, the hour propitious for making bombs, into a game as well. It's a game about the destruction of gamespace—as itself a game. The destruction of gamespace is a game that provides a uniform pleasure with that of any other game. This is the military entertainment complex at its height, constantly displacing boredom into yet more games.

PLAYING *State of Emergency* has a kind of liberating open- [167]
ness. You feel rather than merely see or hear the environment of the game. You scan the mall for weapons, enemies, opportunities. Anything else is just noise. Space is
marked with targets—with boundaries that draw or repel
you according to how they might affect your score and
your progress through the game. The gamer opens out
into the game and is no longer bored. For a bit. But this
openness also has its limits. There's not much to trifle
with, no way to play with style. While in the game and
playing it well, everything in it appears only from the point
of view of its relation to winning the game. Nothing is anything other than a means to that end.

HERE boredom threatens to appear again. You are left [168]
empty by the game, no longer taken (or taken in) by the
things within it. The action appears futile. Nothing moves
you. You opened yourself to the game but the game itself
does not really open toward you. You opened toward something closed. It is an animated space in which things are
just marks of good or bad possibilities within the game.
The possibility of doing anything much seems to be with-
held by the game. It feels like suspended animation. And
yet, strangely, what is frustrating is that possibility itself
seems so tantalizingly tangible precisely because it isn't
here. Something appears precisely because its arrival is
out of bounds. As Heidegger champion Giorgio Agamben
says, it is "the being which exists in the form of potentiality
for being."* But this potential is of a very particular kind. It
is the potential of something no longer particularly hu-

man. It is the potential of topology itself, where your digits, grasping the controller, touch the digital, which in its odd-and-even way touches back.

[169] **GAMESPACE** is an animation machine. The digital and the human lead an uneasy existence there. On the one hand, there are constant attempts to "humanize" the technological, to make it appear as if it were there for you. On the other, it reduces the human to the status of the digital. It marks all of space as a battlespace with yes/no triggers. In *State of Emergency* the human appears to rage against the machine, but the figure of the human within the game is an animation, a machinic special effect. The real human, you might say, is the gamer playing the game. But this human, in order to play, has to think like something other than a human. It has to become animated, a human pretending to be a machine, pretending to be an animal, responding to targets within the game as signals switching on or off behaviors aimed at sheer survival. The gamer coupled with the game is a strange animal.

[170] **HERE IS** some backstory, about a strange, famous animal, known to Heidegger and much discussed since. Deleuze and Guattari: "The tick, attracted by the light, hoists itself up on the tip of a branch; it is sensitive to the smell of mammals, and lets itself fall when one passes beneath the branch; it digs into the skin, at the least hairy place it can find. Just three affects; the rest of the time the tick sleeps, sometimes for years on end, indifferent to all that goes on in the immense forest." It is an animal that lives in a world

of just a few targets. Agamben again: "Under particular circumstances, like those which man creates in laboratories, the animal can effectively suspend its immediate relationship with its environment, without, however, ceasing to be an animal or becoming human." This suspension is also what the digital game does. The gamer suspends a relation with an environment—gamespace—within the special topic of the game, without ceasing to be human or becoming machine.*

YOU KNOW nothing about your body until you know what it [171] can do. Boredom is not doing nothing. Boredom is something a body does when space will not let the body enter it in a way that transforms the body into something else, so that the body can forget itself. Boredom is a suspended animation, but also a suspended self-awareness, made possible by the absence of a certain relation to space, a certain quality of labor. If the triggers in space always point toward the same possibilities, just under different signs, then boredom inevitably returns. *State of Emergency* marks an anxiety within the military entertainment complex about this very possibility. Perhaps it is a game that tries to incorporate and overcome the threat boredom poses to the military entertainment complex by making a game of it. A game which, oddly enough, makes boredom interesting. In a drive-by critique of *State of Emergency*, anti-globalization writer Naomi Klein declares: "Anti-corporate imagery is increasingly being absorbed by corporate marketing."* But the affect runs both ways here. The game might co-opt, but it is at the same time an allegory for an anxiety about what to do when gamespace can no longer collude with boredom. The powers behind the digital might try to co-opt boredom; the boredom of the gamer might yet co-opt the digital instead.

[172] JUST as the military industrial complex once forced the free rhythms of labor into the measured beat of work, so now its successors oblige the free rhythms of play to become equally productive. Alan Liu: "Increasingly, knowledge work has no true recreational outside."* The time and space of the topological world is organized around the maintenance of boredom, nurturing it yet distracting it just enough to prevent its implosion, from which alone might arise the counter power to the game. All the potentials of topology, its lines upon lines, are configured as a gamespace designed to neutralize play and contain it. *State of Emergency* is a game about the possibilities pent up within gamespace. It enacts the game as a repository, a memory, a practice patch for free labor, for autonomous action. It presents this possibility for action as the negation of actually existing gamespace.

[173] THE STRAIGHTFORWARD lines of topographic space left room in the margins for heterotopias which formalized the orders of play. It instituted the chronicles of legends and statistics that would become the game's opening gambit against history. In topographic times, the cyclic repetition of the game never quite reached the threshold of boredom, as there was still an everyday life of work and struggle from which it offered an orderly retreat. The topo-

logical, by contrast, captures all of space in its monotonous grids and all of time in its repetitive innings. Boredom becomes pervasive, uncontainable—a real threat. And so the military entertainment complex invents ever-new games, with new rules, new moves, new chances for competitors to pit themselves against one another, or against chance itself, so as to maintain its grip on the topology it extrudes out of itself, incorporating all of space. Boredom with any particular game is always displaced onto another game, before it calls into question the imperfections of gamespace as a poor excuse for how one could live and labor among these richly productive and seductive lines.

IN TOPOLOGICAL times, play disappears into the game, and [174] boredom looms on all sides. The military entertainment complex responds by introducing into the game every kind of novelty imaginable. Games become less and less a tangible field outside the workaday places of everyday life. They become a gamespace, an intangible tangle of lines along which all information shuttles, subordinated to protocols and rules. Its other scene is no longer a heterotopian playing field as a space and time apart. Rather, it is the atopian space of the digital game, which is more separate from everyday life than a heterotopian playing field but even more of an atopian double for the whole of space itself. The problem with gamespace is not that it relentlessly presents the world via the action of targeting. The problem is that in gamespace things target people, rather than the other way around. It is not that the digital is a technology that cuts into *the world* and presents it to the human as if it were always and already cut to suit us. It is that the digital cuts into *us,* rendering us as bits, and presents those bits to the world made over as a gamespace in which we are the targets.

[175]   THE MILITARY entertainment complex is above all the management and maintenance of boredom. The military wing trains boredom's lax energies outward; the entertainment wing coaches the residual boredom within. Both without and within, boredom is contained within the lines of gamespace. Theologian of play James P. Carse: "The world is elaborately marked by boundaries of contest, its people finely classified as to their eligibilities."* The game plan replaces the work ethic. The interests of the military entertainment complex dominate policy, and policy's goal is to alleviate the threat of boredom. What is good for the military entertainment complex is good for America. And what is pronounced good is the war on boredom, which, like the war on drugs or the war on crime or the war on terror, can never be won—was never meant to be won—and is merely displaced, as the boredom index rises and falls. For boredom can arise anywhere and everywhere, once space is made over as topology. The trick for the military entertainment complex is to collude in maintaining boredom, without having it turn upon it and bite the feed that powers all our distractions.

# COMPLEX

(on *Deus Ex*)

THERE ARE four ways in which the topology of gamespace can come to an end and be superseded by a new topos—at least according to the game *Deus Ex: Invisible War*. (If you've played this game, you may know there is also a fifth ending, of which protocol demands the withholding until the puzzle of the other four endings unlocks its significance.) In the game, your character has to choose between aiding the victory of one of four organizations, all of which are at odds with one another, and each of which has its own idea of how to realize a permanent atopia beyond gamespace, a topos beyond topology. Working backward from these four endings, one can plot the backstory not just of *Deus Ex* but of the military entertainment complex—at least as it can be understood from within the game, from within The Cave itself.*

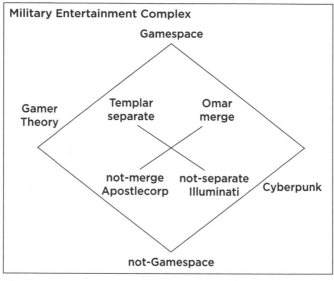

**Fig. G**

〖177〗 THE FOUR endings of *Deus Ex* can be pieced together by arranging them in two pairs (see Fig. G). The first, more "personal" pair of endings pits the victory of the Templars against that of the Omar. The Templars are a fanatical religious order devoted to the body's purification of all "biomods." The Omar are a no less fearsome collective organism of black marketeers, in which the body has been subsumed into technology. The second, more "political" pair of endings pits the victory of the Illuminati against that of ApostleCorp. The Illuminati are a secret cabal of power-brokers hidden behind organizational fronts, dedicated to restoring order under their control. ApostleCorp is a techno-intellectual faction dedicated to bringing about a just and democratic but no less "posthuman" civilization. You, the gamer, play a minor character who can nevertheless tip the balance between these powers and their goals.

DEUS EX is a shadowy world. Some of the organizations [178] who at first appear so powerful are just fronts for others. For instance the neoliberal WTO and the religious fundamentalists of The Order, which appear antagonistic to each other in every way, turn out—in classic conspiracy theory style—to be but masks secretly controlled by the Illuminati. This chain of unmasking can be extended even beyond the game. Behind the final four powers—Templar and Omar, Illuminati and ApostleCorp—is at least one more unmasking. The first pair of endings—Templar and Omar—masks an agon between the complete assimilation of the human into the machine (Omar) versus the complete rejection of the intercourse of body with machine (Templar). Along this axis, the problem of where gamespace is heading is "personal," a question of the boundaries of the body and its other. The other pair of endings—Illuminati and ApostleCorp—is less about the immediate relation of body to machine as something personal—it is about something not personal, something that is perhaps political. Here the ends of gamespace are an agon between the "democratic," in which all bodies communicate equally with machines, versus the hierarchical, where all communication passes via a controlling power. The personal is political, but in *Deus Ex* the impersonal is political, too.

[179] FOR THE gamer, it's always a matter of starting at the beginning and playing through to the end. In the original *Deus Ex* and its sequel, *Invisible War*, there are different ways of getting from beginning to end.* It can be done by stealth, by violence, or by negotiation, but either way the game reveals itself level by level, from start to finish. For the gamer as theorist, perhaps in *Deus Ex* it's a matter of taking the end as the starting point. The question of what can constitute an end state is the question of what occupies the limits to thought within gamespace. Why these four endings? If they are just arbitrary, random possibilities, then they may be fun for the gamer to play through but not much fun for the gamer theorist to start out from in this other game—the game of exploring the relation between the allegorithm of the game to the allegory of gamespace. But perhaps the four endings of *Deus Ex* are not random but are rather the pieces of a puzzle.

[180] BEHIND the four organizations who vie for power in *Invisible War* are four more abstract, more impersonal antagonists who stalk the fantastic vistas of gamespace itself. Either technology trumps the human or vice versa (Templar vs. Omar). Either democracy trumps hierarchy or vice versa (Illuminati vs. ApostleCorp). But beyond that, perhaps the game reaches a certain limit. Behind this mask is not another mask; behind this power is not another power, but something else—a diagram of the avatars of power. The four endings exhaust the possibilities within which gamespace can think about itself. They are its endgame. But while there is not at this point another charac-

ter to unmask, there is a puzzle to solve in the arrangement of these masks. These endings, and what they mask, enter into quite definite relations. The four terms invite the gamer theorist to a new kind of game.

THE FOUR possible endings of *Deus Ex* fit on a "Greimas square." Which is to say, the endings are terms in a game of meaning-making (see Fig. G). If George Perec is the avant garde aesthete of gamespace, Greimas is its pioneering theorist, for whom all culture can now be thought of retrospectively in terms of the game. A. J. Greimas: "Perhaps out of a desire for intelligibility, we can imagine that, in order to achieve the construction of cultural objects (literary, mythical, pictorial, etc.), the human mind begins with simple elements and follows a complex trajectory, encountering on its way both constraints to which it must submit and choices it is able to make."* Or in other words, the play of meaning is made within the bounds of a game. At stake here is the relation of play to game. As topography gives way to topology, the game rises in prominence relative to play. In the realm of avant garde strategies, the game-within-constraints of George Perec trumps the play-beyond-game of Guy Debord. In the rear guard of theoretical strategies, the game of meaning supersedes the meaning of games; A. J. Greimas tops Johan Huizinga. For Huizinga, play precedes game. It is the play "instinct" that inspires the formation of forms. Greimas anticipates the enclosure of play within gamespace. As the whole of space succumbs to the game, it is the logic of constraints that determines the possibilities of play.

[182] HUIZINGA, writing in the shadow of the Nazis, knew what was coming: "It remained for the theory of 'total war' to . . . extinguish the last vestige of the play element." The military industrial complex was on its way. Total war then extended its logistics to the spaces of work and finally to play itself. Now the military entertainment complex was on its way. Transgressive play had its last hurrah in the Situationist attempt to live out Huizinga's theory as a program for action. Greil Marcus: "As bathos it was just drunks trying to walk and think at the same time." There was nowhere to hide outside of gamespace—the total game. Guy Debord: "One cannot go into exile in a unified world." The former leader of the Situationists devoted his declining years to designing and playing a board game that formalized all he imagined he had learned about revolutionary playtime, and yet entombed it within its rules.*

[183] WITH THE rise of topology, the tension between game and play was resolved in favor of the game. Whether in art, theory, or in everyday life, there was nothing outside the game. The storyline, which once marked the boundaries within which a game could begin, became internal to gamespace, and was now much more about legitimizing the point at which a game "must" begin and end. The storyline became just the working out, one move at a time, of a possible line through the constraints of gamespace. In the game it was an algorithm that determined when something could end; but it was the storyline that made this end point seem natural, inevitable, and necessary. But while a storyline has an ending, *Deus Ex* has four endings. It re-

veals just a bit more of the rules of the game of meaning-making than a story usually would. That *Deus Ex* is a game of four endings is already a slight slippage of the mask, revealing the rules of the meaning-making game.

**IN TOPOGRAPHIC** times, heterotopian games opened onto [184] nongame spaces. A game was delineated by what it was not. In topological times, atopian games opened onto nothing but other games. In gamespace, the exit from one game turns out to be an entry into another. Each cave lets onto another cave. But this does not banish the problem of what is not-game. On the contrary, it makes it a pervasive and incessant problem. Its locus is the gamer, who can only be a gamer by being constantly pulled into and pushed out of one game after another, and who, in moments of boredom in between, glimpses the very conditions of possibility in gamespace. These are the moments when the gamer can neither target something within the game nor be the target the game itself selects to make its own. The tension is no longer what is prior to or outside the game but what, from inside the game, may bring it to an end—and what that end might be.

**THE GAMER'S** boredom arises out of the recognition that, [185] under the variegated spectacle of details, the act of gaming is always essentially the same. The gamer oscillates between two states. The first state is being separate from the target; the second is being merged with the target. (Playing *Deus Ex* in stealth mode only reverses the procedure. The goal is to not be the other's target.) The first state merges the gamer with the character in the presence of the target, the second merges the character with the target and produces, as a result, the gamer, as the one who hit or missed (see Fig. F). The gamer oscillates within an agon between two terms: being separate and being merged into the game. In *Deus Ex,* the Templars are the knights of separation; the Omar want nothing but complete synthesis of human and machine. This first pair in the Greimas square enact the realization of the game as one of two agonistic states in which the gamer may be in relation to any game.

[186] ONE MAY be Omar or Templar, merged or separated from gamespace, but this pair of terms masks another: beyond the antagonistic positions of being merged or separated, there is a pair of slightly different terms, which are other to the initial pair rather than antagonistic to them. You may be separate or merged; but you may also be not-separate or not-merged. This latter pair of possibilities opens up a lot more territory. The antagonist of separate is merged, but the other of separate is the not-separate, which could be many other states. The antagonist of merged is separate, but the other of merged is not-merged, which could be many other states. Within the game, the agonistic seems to define a digital difference: if not one thing, then another. One term antagonizes another term, each of which defines the other negatively. Each is what the other is not. But in the relation of game to not-game, the relation to the other term takes precedence. A game always depends on a prior difference, not quite digital but of another order. This is otherness, wherein a term is posited against a pure negative, against what is not it. This other term does not in turn

draw its identity from this relation. It remains unmarked. A game begins by ruling out what is not-game. It says nothing about what not-game is. There is nothing it can say about what not-game is. Nor can it say where not-game begins or ends.

TO BE not-separate from the game could be many things. [187] From within the logic of the game, the only way to venture into this territory is by positing something that can go in the place of the not-separate. The game expands here under the guise of the Illuminati. Perhaps there is something beyond the digital, on-off relation of the gamer with the game. Perhaps it is bigger than that. Perhaps there are protocols determining who has access to which game; perhaps some games are more important than other games and determine the possible outcomes of subordinate games. Even more disturbing: Perhaps you only appear to be the player of a game. Perhaps you are really a "non-player character" in a game controlled by someone or something else. Perhaps if you took off your own mask, the mask of the gamer, you would find that you only imagine yourself to be the one playing—perhaps you are the one who has been played. Ice T: "You played yourself."* In a gamespace governed by protocol, by codes of access and denial of access, to one thing fronted or not fronted by another, every appearance prompts the paranoid suspicion that it is not what it seems.

TO BE not-merged with the game might also be a more [188] complex term than either the merged or separate terms. Holding down its place is ApostleCorp. Perhaps it is not about more or less separation. Perhaps it is a qualitative relation that can't be captured by the simple terms of separation and merger, nor yet by the protocols and hierarchies of the not-separate. Here you may find the ghost of Huizinga, and a play that calls into being its own rules. This fourth term may be the most interesting of all, but one that is usually suppressed in favor of one of the other three. Nevertheless, the fourth term has to find its place in the puzzle in order to unlock the next level in this game.

[189] **THE FIRST** storyline strand—from Templar to Illuminati— starts with the separation of gamer and game, and terror about merging human and machine. But beyond this existential tension, the storyline develops the thought of what can be outside of separation and merger. It fantasizes a power of control over the relation between separation and merger. The merger at the basest levels is presided over by a separation at the top. Or vice versa: Separation at the bottom resists and reacts against merger at the top.

[190] **THE SECOND** storyline—from Omar to ApostleCorp—takes the opposite path. It also begins with the existential question of the separation of gamer and game, or of the human and the nonhuman. Only it resolves the tension in favor not of separation but of merger. It takes merger for granted. This is the properly "cyberpunk" axis. It starts with the assumption of a schizoid splitting and mixing of layers and levels of flesh and metal. The storyline axis then travels toward the fourth term, which is that of the nonmerger. Are there ways for the soft machine of the body

and the digital machine of the game to coexist? On what terms? Could there be a communication between them? A communication in which one need not be the antagonist of the other? Deleuze and Guattari: "The schizophrenic is the universal producer. There is no need to distinguish here between producing and its product. We need merely note that the pure 'thisness' of the object produced is carried over into a new act of producing."* It might not be an antagonism of opposites, still less a communication of equivalents, so much as an excitation of incommensurables, of flesh by machine and machine by flesh.

THE TEMPLAR attract the sense of panic (and resignation) [149] about the machine; the Omar a fear (and euphoria) that it is too late and that any dalliance with the digital subsumes anything human. The Illuminati open toward a paranoia about what might be behind gamespace: a mysterious conspiracy and perhaps a critical theory—of the military entertainment complex. The fourth term points towards a digital delirium, a negated realm of possibilities—an "extopian" possibility, in which gamer and game cease to exist as separate terms, and there is a complete elimination of the limits of any topos. The extopian dwells neither here nor there but at once and at one with the world. The possible endings of *Deus Ex* map out the topos of the military entertainment complex. It is a synthesis of the two competing storylines that try to account for everyday life from within The Cave, or what some call the "posthuman condition." Katherine Hayles: "The prospect of becoming posthuman evokes terror and excites pleasure."* Perhaps in equal measure, and always at the same time.

[192] THE FOUR endings of *Deus Ex* play out all of these possibilities. The agonistic forces of the Templars and the Omar open toward what they are not, but in place of what they are not, the game posits another pair of antagonistic terms—Illuminati and ApostleCorp. This second pair stage the agonistic storylines of the paranoid complex and a schizoid complexity. For the Templars, separation is key, and yet to fight in this posthuman grid, they require technics, armor for example, which implicates them in various forms of non-separation from the very thing their being is founded on separation from. For the Omar, the problem is the reverse. Theirs is a being not defined by an assumption of an always already separate being—a gamer before the game who might have anxiety about its boundaries, about tripping into the nonhuman. They are always already not human. Yet they have to find ways to communicate with what *is* human, with what is separate, in order to draw it into the game. At either end of this agon, of complete merger or complete separation, the problem looks like one of another difference—non-separation, non-merger. But this other difference is now internal to the game. Gamespace has colonized what it is not, and erected in its place a new agon. It subordinates the analog to the digital.

[193] START over. Here are the rules of the game: Start with an agon of Templar vs. Omar. Find the values masked by these proper names (separate vs. merged). Discover the hidden exclusion masked by these terms (not-separate vs. not-merged). Detect the positive terms which cover the ab-

sence of these pure negations (Illuminati vs. ApostleCorp). Now for the next level: Does gamespace stop there? Or is it not always a double masking—of the value masked by the character, and of the indeterminate negativity masked by an agon of positive terms? After unmasking the Illuminati as a mere cover for non-separation, what next? Do these masks cover and cover to infinity? Here another dimension reveals itself. Are these masks of characters for values, and of values for negations, not the protocols to a total game? Starting from the Templars, these are the questions one might pose in the act of gameplay, which might work out the terms of the conspiracy by which the complex hides itself, but not so completely that a paranoid sensibility might not puzzle it out.

START over again. Start instead from the Omar. What is [194] behind them? The value of a complete merger of gamer and game. But what might a non-merger be? Could this relation of not only gamer to game but of gamers to games be otherwise? Could a more intimate relation of gamer to game yet be the condition of possibility for the autonomous self-creation of something beyond the gamer? And of something beyond the game? Starting from the Omar, this is the territory in which you might find yourself. This is the terrain of a schizoid blurring of the boundaries of flesh and machine, opening not toward a complex of control but a complexity beyond all centralizing forms of power. Rather than the digital boundary, separating gamer from game, here it is an analog relation, a variable relation of gamer into game.

[195] *DEUS* *Ex* opens the problem of the other behind the agon of positive terms—and closes it again. But in this closing, it provides the place for a gamer theory to start a new kind of game. Or rather, it provides two places—and the possibility of two kinds of gamer theory. The first could be called critical, or perhaps just paranoid. From the Templar's agon with the Omar, we ignore the Omar for a moment and think instead of the Templar's relation to the Illuminati, which stands revealed as a positive term masking the point of a negation, that of the not-separate. This revelation of a pure negative, where it is not given what the other term is, opens toward a paranoid sensibility, which is where the possibility of a critical thought pointing beyond the game might lie. Sigmund Freud: "The delusions of paranoiacs have an unpalatable external similarity and internal kinship to the systems of philosophers."* The paranoia of the not-separate is in not knowing what you are not-separate from. Paranoid thought always seeks out the powers that hide in the shadows of the not-separate.

[196] START over. Start instead from the Omar. Ignoring for the moment their agon with the Templars, consider instead the Omar's other relation to ApostleCorp, who are posited in the place of the not-merged. But here might lie a quite different possibility for a gamer theory—not paranoid but schizoid. Rather than ask an analyst like Freud about the power of negation, if you ask a patient, particularly a patient who defeated the game, perhaps one gets a different answer, a schizo's analysis. Heretical Surrealist Antonin Artaud: "Which indeed is not a philosophy, but in the pan

of fried potatoes, square perhaps with the handle of the cantilever which bears like the spoon in the perforated tongue of the sex organ forever denied by the heart."* To the paranoid sensibility, what appears positively—as one's antagonist—masks what is negative. It masks not-being. Everything appears as a fight to the end, unmasking one after another as false positivities, each yielding over and over to nothingness, always seeking the face of total power masked behind not-being. To the schizoid sensibility, on the other hand, undoing the agon between one positivity and other opens up more positive differences, positivity to infinity, and a perverse play of terms outside any storyline demarking being from not being. The problem with schizos is that they take words for things; the problem with paranoiacs is that they take things for words.

BOTH choices offered for a gamer theory have their limita- [197] tions. One starts with separation from the game and opens toward conspiracy theories, and perhaps toward a critical theory of separation. This move suppresses atopia without realizing it. The other starts with the merger of gamer into game and opens toward a cyberpunk celebration of the hybridity of nervous system and circuit board. This move realizes atopia without suppressing it. The rise of gamespace may conclude with either the suppression and realization of the game—and the gamer. What could be the endgame of gamespace itself? Who—or what—can come after the persona of the gamer? How can you both suppress and realize the game? How could one come to live in a topos in which one's actions can be freely chosen and yet

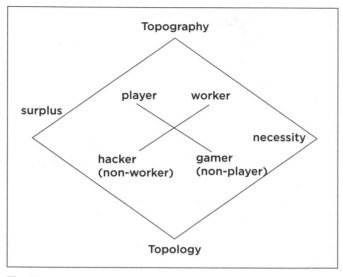

Fig. H

not insignificant? How could one be both free from necessity yet unsullied by boredom? How could one be neither a prisoner of work nor condemned to a merely frivolous play? This is what is at stake in the game.

[198] **ANOTHER** Greimas square: Childish play is antagonistic to the serious business of work. Player vs. worker. But who stands in the place of the non-player? The gamer. The gamer is outside of but not the opposite of the player. But who then is the non-worker? Let's call this character the hacker (see Fig. H). To hack is outside of but not opposite to work. It is a free, self-directed activity that makes its own rules, its own conditions of completion, and its own protocols of success. It is an algorithm that writes itself. It

is a practice beyond work and play, and against the game, and which calls for another character. Here is the mask of the fourth character: "We are the hackers of abstraction. We produce new concepts, new perceptions, new sensations, hacked out of raw data. Whatever code we hack, be it programming language, poetic language, math or music, curves or colorings, we are the abstracters of new worlds."* The character of the hacker is what is worshipped in that new category of celebrity, the game designer. If the celebrities of play were transgressors of rules, the celebrities of the game are makers of rules—but only within certain constraints. Not even the game designer gets to make the rules of gamespace. Not even an Information Overlord like the CEO of Electronic Arts, Larry Probst. What would it mean to be a hacker not just of games but of gamespace itself? This is the realized atopia that AppostleCorp stands for.

IN *DEUS Ex: Invisible War* the name for what is at the center of this universe of futures is Helios. This sun around which all revolves is said to be—like Eden in *Rez*—an "artificial intelligence" but is in effect a game engine, and what is at stake is the relation, via this game engine, of the gamer with the game. A game engine is a maker of worlds, but of worlds that appear as if they were made for the gamer, as if they lent themselves to actions that could uncover their protocols. While other media present the world as if it were for you to look at, the game engine presents worlds as if they were not just for you to look at but for you to act upon in a way that is given. The realm of the not-game is the domain in which the gamer cannot act as a gamer. The separation of the game from the not-game creates this space of possible perceptions and actions.

[200] *DEUS Ex* has a fifth ending, nested inside the game, where all of its characters, regardless of rank or faction, get down and party. Here is the limit to gamespace within gamespace itself, where differences lack antagonism, and yet for all that do not cease to be differences. Terms coexist without reduction to one vs. another. Could there be a topos after topology that is not a regression back to the topographic or even the topical? Could there be an overcoming of necessity that does not dissipate into useless boredom? Could the gamer come into possession of the means to make the rule as well as the move? Could the gamer also be a hacker, a maker of rules for moves as well as of moves within rules? This is the threshold to which *Deus Ex* brings us. But if there is a deus ex machina at work in this game, it is the one that rescues the game itself from its own overcoming. Even the fifth ending, which could point to a conclusion beyond the game, merely posits another one, where characters masquerade like celebrities and the gamer feels privileged to have slipped behind the velvet rope.

# CONCLUSIONS
## (on *SimEarth*)

**Y**OU ARRIVE home from work one evening, only to discover your biosphere is dead. What a way to start the week! On looking back through the records, the reason is not hard to discover. A classic greenhouse-effect problem. Next time, wind down the fossil fuels a little more so your globe doesn't cook itself to death while you're out. Fortunately, the biosphere in question is only a game, or something like a game. You have this program running on your home computer called *SimEarth*, which lets you model all kinds of biosphere conditions over a number of different time frames: geological, biological, and sociological.* The one you think you're getting a little obsessed with is a model of planet Earth from 1990 onward. So this week you decide that you'll set up this model every morning, selecting types and quantities of energy use and expenditure. You'll come home every evening and see if your world is still running. Sometimes it is, sometimes it isn't.

[202] **THERE'S** something a little eerie about having a functioning biosphere in your home; something rather more disturbing about finding the thing has gone belly-up while you were out at work. *SimEarth* lets you choose from a number of energy sources, including biomass, hydroelectric, solar, nuclear, or fossil fueled. It also lets you program a range of energy uses, including science, agriculture, medicine, and the arts. Each of these has different effects. If you expend energy on agriculture, population increases rather more rapidly. If you devote more resources to science, technological change accelerates. Some of the assumptions here are of course crude, but not unreasonable. Naturally, a home biosphere has to run a relatively simple algorithm compared to the heavy-duty model.

[203] **THE CURIOUS** thing about it is how fiddling around with these crude variables gives you a feel for the global impact of fundamental choices about what economists call *resource allocation*. For instance, you start it up one midweek morning with settings that devote a lot of resources to agriculture. This seems a reasonable approach to creating a minimalist atopia. Theodor Adorno: "There is tenderness only in the coarsest demand: that no-one should go hungry any more. Every other seeks to apply to a condition that ought to be determined by human needs, a mode of conduct adapted to production as an end in itself."* And yet it doesn't quite work out. When you come home from work

you find the population shot through the roof. That one was predictable. What you hadn't counted on, though, was that increasing agriculture pumped out more green-house gasses. The temperature was ever so slowly rising, threatening to toast everything, unevenly but very crisply brown. And all because of that troubling phrase "human needs" . . .

LIKE any patient confronted with a terminal diagnosis, you [204] wanted a second opinion. So you set *SimEarth* running at home before driving off to work, where you steal a little time to fire up your browser and go web surfing in good old-fashioned cyberspace. The urgent problem is to find out why increasing the amount of food being grown has this lethal effect. The prognosis is not good. It seems that methane is one of the gasses that causes global warming. A bit too much methane in the air and heat gets trapped in the atmosphere. By dialing up more agriculture, you also upped the amount of methane going into the atmosphere. Rice paddies, for instance, are one of the sources of meth-ane. It seems that deep in the muck at the bottom of rice paddies are little bacteria that produce methane as a by-product. Great! There you were, only this morning trying to see to it that all the people on your biosphere are getting enough to eat, and by the time you come home for dinner you're cooking the biosphere.

THIS is all a bit too much, but fortunately the next day is the [205] end of the working week and you are going out to dinner afterward with friends. You imagine this might take your mind off *SimEarth*, but all that food on the table makes you lose your appetite. That big silvery dish with all that rice in it smells like over-cooked biosphere. The beef, delicious though it tastes, only makes things worse. It seems that one of the other sources of methane in the world is, of all things, cow farts. Yes, cow farts. It never occurred to you that there was the slightest global significance in the fact that cows are a bit gassy. The problem is, they fart (and belch) methane. Well, not the cows exactly, but the bacteria in their stomachs that break down all that feed. Those bacteria, like their teeming little prokaryote relatives in the rice paddies, also make methane.

[206] **THE WEEKEND** comes, so now you can really spend some time on this biosphere business. When you programmed your little biosphere with lots of food production so that nobody would go hungry, you also selected a higher rate of methane output. It just goes to show how you have to think about all of the consequences of anything you do. That nobody should go hungry is a worthy goal, but, *all things being equal,* it means more people, and more people means more land under cultivation, and that means more methane, and that is a bit of a problem. So the next time you set up *SimEarth,* you do things a bit differently. Rather than concentrate on expanding food production in the short term, why not put more resources into science and technology instead? This is a bit of a gamble, you think to yourself as you drive off to the mall in your high-tech hybrid car, the kind Al Gore recommends.* What if science didn't come up with the answers in time? What if burn-

ing up fossil fuels didn't kick progress along fast enough? What if people go hungry? What the hell is progress anyway?

**BY THE** time you return home, *SimEarth* has reverted to [207] what it calls, with a certain drollery, "geological time." There is nothing left alive, so your planet is just ticking over, waiting quartz eons for life to mysteriously spark again. What happened? Check the charts. Let's see: pollution up, oxygen levels down, carbon dioxide up, temperatures sky high. It seems the techno-gamble didn't quite work out. Cranking up the whole global economy to the max, pumping out and burning up every source of energy as fast as possible certainly did increase the pace of technological change, but in this scenario it increased the rate of global climate change even faster.

**THE PROBLEM** wasn't the methane this time. By keeping [208] population and food production growing a bit more slowly it seems you kept your little green earth from spinning out into that fate. The problem this time was the carbon dioxide. There it is on the graph—shooting up at a devilishly sharp tack, taking temperatures up with it. Burning fossil fuels—oil and coal—produces carbon dioxide, among other things, and when you increase the amount of carbon dioxide in the atmosphere, you turn the toaster on again. Like methane, it traps the heat from sunlight. The really sad part is that all the way home in the car from your trip to the mall, loaded up with organic vegetables, biodegradable toilet paper, and the new slim-line model

PlayStation, you had been really eager to see if your little gamble had paid off.

[209] YOU HAD not quite absorbed the idea that driving is part of the problem. Marx showed how each act of concrete, specific, particular labor is made equivalent, by the wage relation, to every other. Concrete labor is also abstract labor. In gamespace, every concrete, specific action of any kind is also an abstract action, the consuming of a given resource for a given result. And yet gamespace does not encompass and account for every action. Only those inputs that take the form of an agon between competing forces in the market can be calculated. But behind the agon lies a host of other terms, shading off into the imperceptible, that comes back to taunt gamespace with its cumulative effect. What sets *SimEarth* apart is that the unintended consequences of agon, all these other excluded outputs, received at least an approximate accounting.

[210] YOU HAD always thought that if the economy in the real world cranked along at maximum efficiency, then technology would also bobble along at a rate sufficient to deal with the little problems that might occur along the way. Just like in a well-designed game. Karl Marx: "Mankind thus inevitably sets itself only such tasks as it is able to solve, since closer examination will always show that the problem itself arises only when the material conditions for its solution are already present or at least in the course of formation."* Well, maybe. What the *SimEarth* allegorithm points to is that like most people, you had always taken this on faith. What happens if the little problems aren't just accidental

byproducts—a little oil spill here, a toxic waste disaster there—what if the military entertainment complex itself was mucking up the global conditions of its own success? Gamespace is just like your PlayStation. It appears to itself as a rigorous game, with every action accounted for, and yet it relies on a huge power cord poking out the back that sucks in energy from an elsewhere for which it makes no allowance. That the game is not really ruled off from the world, that it relies on an external source of power, did not really occur to you until you played your new PlayStation for hours and hours and it overheated. Tantalum, like the rest of planet earth, is only good with so much heat. There is something outside The Cave after all. Game over.

ALL RIGHT, so maybe third time lucky. Let's ease up on the [211] agricultural output and the use of fossil fuels. Here's an idea: let's go nuclear! Maybe this is the way to have the best of both worlds, so to speak. Lots of energy to keep industry and technology cooking, but without turning on the big heat of the greenhouse toaster-oven. Run it overnight and test your nuclear gambit. Sunday morning comes. Well, this time there is good news and bad news. The good news: your biosphere didn't cook this time. You have well and truly solved the greenhouse problem—permanently. The bad news: Rather than overheat it, you accidentally shoved it into the deep freeze. It's called "nuclear winter," and it results from letting off a few too many thermonuclear devices. The dust cloud from that keeps the sunlight out altogether. Cormac McCarthy: "Like the onset of some cold glaucoma dimming away the world."*

[212] BY CLICKING on the nuclear option, you gave your little SimEarthlings not only a great source of power but a dangerous weapon. It was not as if you had taken away the sources of potential conflict, however. Conditions were not exactly ripe, it seems, for global consciousness. A. A. Bogdanov: "The struggle between classes, groups, and individuals precludes both the idea of the whole and the happiness and suffering implied by the notion." They just started blasting away at each other. Perhaps they didn't invent game theory, and figure out that deterrence works only if nobody shoots. And perhaps that's your fault—you reduced inputs for science and culture. The radioactive patches on the surface of this digital earth burn through a few eons-worth of the subsequent "geological" phase. You can see little nuke signs appear on the brown stump of a formerly green planet, like vandal-carved graffiti on trees that announces to nobody in particular: *We were here.* How did this happen? While the now quite visible hand of agon within gamespace metes out resources according to its law, an invisible foot, composed of all that shades away into mere indistinct otherness, qualities without quantities, kicks it to pieces. You lose again. Kim Stanley Robinson: "It was frightening—as if history were a series of human wave assaults on misery, failing time after time."*

[213] IT'S NOT much of a game, *SimEarth*. Perhaps that's why after seven days of uncreation, you became bored with it. Then uninstalled it. Then finally got around to selling it on eBay. Perhaps I bought your old copy. I played it for a while, on an obsolete computer. It can get a little obsessive.

*SimEarth* gamers tell amazing stories—about the time the lid blew off the biosphere but up rose a strain of intelligent robots. Or the time it ticked over for months, populated with a million sentient cetaceans, all using nanotechnology to run their watery utopia. But there's something disturbing about it. Perhaps that's why there is no sequel, no updates. It is as extinct an example of game evolution as the poor Simcritters who populate its sun-blasted endgames. *SimEarth* is extinct, a game without sequels, but two offshoots from the same evolutionary phyla of game design lived on. One is *The Sims.* Perhaps it was better adapted to survive in gamespace because it did not give the game away. The death of a Sim is not the end of the world. Another descendant line tries the other tack. In Will Wright's much admired *Spore,* survival is not limited to one biosphere. Olaf Stapeldon: "It must not be supposed that the normal fate of intelligent races in the galaxy is to triumph."* At least in *Spore* there's more than one home to trash.

FORMS of games evolve in a quasi-Darwinian manner, not [214] unlike forms of organisms. Game designers breed new forms out of existing forms, and the military entertainment complex throws the resulting variations on a waiting market, where they compete to save you from boredom. Very few forms succeed. It's almost Darwinian: The designer proposes; gamespace disposes. Franco Moretti: "In Darwin, in other words, history is the interweaving of *two* wholly independent paths: random variation and necessary selection. In our case, [formal] innovations, which are the result of chance, and a social selection, which by contrast is the daughter of necessity."* Through a subtle inversion of the logic of natural selection, gamespace claims to be the full implementation of a digital Darwinism. Here for one and all the rule is *survival of the fittest.* Only what actually happens is quite the reverse: the demise of the unfit. Survival has no positive value. Gamespace is a pure nihilism. The best one can hope for is merely being undefeated. Hence, the unsatisfying quality of "winning" in *SimEarth.* In the unlikely event that the game rattles on toward the death of the sun, this victory amounts to nothing. This is perhaps why *SimEarth* did not survive. There is something too painful in this game of worldly cruelty. But there is a difference between natural selection and "cultural" selection. An "unfit" game like *SimEarth* fails not because it bumps up against the reality principle of bare life, but quite the reverse. It fails the fantasy principle.

[215]   GIVEN that you can't really win, *SimEarth* is hardly a game at all. The best conclusion for most scenarios is that your SimEarthlings leave the planet in a fleet of spaceships. *SimEarth* lacks one of the usual criteria for a game—what we might call a satisfying "win condition" that terminates its algorithm. But then perhaps that's the allegory. *SimEarth* maps the limit of gamespace. What gamespace usually excludes—the residues that pile up out-of-sight out-of-mind—are here included, and they are the source of the problem. The choices within the game—between agriculture and science, for example—appear as choices between positive terms. They take no account of their un-

namable others, which appear unmarked. How are we to think of non-science, of non-agriculture? *SimEarth's* strategy is to include every term within its agon. There is no other, or almost none. It posits the whole planet as gamespace. Even the power source of the sun is included. Only the blank space interstellar of the angels remains as its other.*

THE INCLUSION of almost everything within the game [216] leaves little by way of a topos in which to conquer, expand, colonize, transform. Sure you could terraform Mars, but the result seems a foregone conclusion. There is no frontier along which a storyline might traffic the unknown into the realm of the known. A certain kind of history ends here. Says the Stalinist-Surrealist poet Paul Eluard: "There is another world, and it is this one." *SimEarth* closes the book on that utopian realm, and on the struggle for and against it. Gamespace has consumed the world, but the catastrophe of the world's consummation comes back to taunt it, undoing it from within. E. M. Cioran: "There is no other world. Nor even this one."* Once all terms are included within the agon of gamespace, the whole of life becomes a game that can be lost, forever.

SIMEARTH is by genre a "God game." Some God! Again and [217] again, you fail your creation. *SimEarth* is not so much about the death of God as God's suicide. It takes away the *empowering* thought of being responsible for His disposal. Here suicide is either fast and violent, in which God throws himself into the flames of global warming. Or very,

very slow—hooked, like a helpless junkie, to the sun. A sun that finally overcomes your ability to *maintain*. Mark Amerika: "Oblivion is the only cure for agony."* The delusion of God games is that the gamer is in control when at the controller. *I'm the decider!* But it is the game that plays the gamer. It is you, the gamer, who is an avatar, in the sense of being the incarnation of an abstract principle. The gamer is a lesser deity incarnate, answerable to a higher power—the game itself.

[218]    WHEN gamespace chooses you as its avatar, which character does it select for you to play? Perhaps in *SimEarth* the gamer is the avatar of the Angel of History. Walter Benjamin: "Where a chain of events appears before us, he sees only one single catastrophe, which keeps piling wreckage upon wreckage and hurls it at his feet. The angel would like to stay, awaken the dead, and make whole what has been smashed. But a storm is blowing from paradise and has got caught in his wings; it is so strong that the angel can no longer close them." Or perhaps you are an avatar of the Luckless Angel, with rather different hitpoints. Heiner Müller: "The past surges behind him, pouring rubble on wings and shoulders thundering like buried drums, while in front of him the future collects, crushes his eyes, exploding his eyeballs like a star wrenching the word into a resounding gag, strangling him with its breath." This suits the experience—and the times—rather better. The droll experience of being flung forward into nothingness by the terminal transformation of nature; an experience of truth as hell seen too late. *SimEarth* is an allegory of the ends of

gamespace, which declares its victory over the gamer and over any other residue of contraries outside its form of forms. It pops the blue eye of the gamer's world.*

PERHAPS you are an avatar of the Egyptian demigod [219] Theuth, who according to Plato was the inventor of not only writing but also number and calculation, geometry and astronomy, games of chance and games of skill. In a story Socrates tells in *Phaedrus,* Theuth offers these to the king Thamus and says: "What I have discovered [are recipes] of memory and wisdom." Thamus, the sun-God, the ultimate authority, key to the great chain of being, who speaks for being itself, considers the gifts of Theuth one by one. In Socrates' telling, it is writing about which Thamus has the most qualms. For the problems of memory, recording, delineating, is this recipe, or "pharmakon," of writing a remedy or a poison? Writing sends the word—logos—out into the world estranged from the authority of its author, erasing the line of its paternity, making of it an orphan. In this sense, it's a father-killing poison, and it would make of Thamus the sun-god a marked man. But the sungod only has to give the word. Behind writing lies speech, and behind speech, the pure light of the good. Jacques Derrida: "The good (father, sun, capital) is thus the hidden illuminating, blinding source of logos." Thamus refuses Theuth's gifts. But perhaps that's not the end of the story.*

PERHAPS what Theuth had to offer Thamus was not [220] recipes but algorithms. Manuel De Landa: "These recipes . . . include rules of thumb and shortcuts discovered by trial and error, useful habits of mind developed through experience, and tricks of the trade passed on from one generation of problem-solvers to the next. Some of the valuable insights . . . may then be captured in a general purpose, 'infallible' problem solving recipe (known as an 'algorithm')."* And what if Theuth had killed Thamus and taken his place? What if it were not writing but *all* Theuth's algorithms that were his power? The algorithms of writing, calculation, navigation, and the game, at first separately and then coming together, create a topology, a world no longer logocentric but ludocentric. Theuth sets himself up as King Digital. Behind appearances lies a new Helios, the artificial sun-king of the algorithm, able to name, locate, value, calculate, and set in play anything and everything but the sun itself. If in Plato history moves between mythos and logos, it comes finally to rest between logos and ludus, between writing and the game, in a world where the originary power of voice is neither here nor there. The sun that powers *SimEarth*, the light which illuminates The Cave, is not the sun-god Thamus but the algorithms of Theuth. But by this light, *SimEarth* tells the inconvenient truth about gamespace—that it can know its limit, its end, but not what to do about it.

[221] TRULY, as the schizo-prophet Antonin Artaud foresaw, by installing gamespace in and as the world, we woke the Gods who sleep in museums. Gamespace changes the nature of historical time, provoking backward glances to the certainties of myth. Game time may be either geological, biological, or sociological, but it is no longer historical.

History is *history*. Or rather, a certain conception and a certain practice is history. History can no longer be a storyline about free agency constructing its own conditions of existence. Fredric Jameson: "History is what hurts, it is what refuses desire and sets inexorable limits to individual as well as collective praxis." In gamespace, history is where random variation meets necessary selection. The game is what grinds. It shapes its gamers, not in its own image but according to its algorithms. The passage from topic to topography to topology is the passage from myth storyline to gamespace, from voice to text to code. In its last stages, this transformation, this "progress," takes us from analog control of the digital to digital control of the analog, from the diachronic sequence of events to the synchronic intercommunications of space, from voice to code. Perhaps history reappears, but at a more synthetic, even photosynthetic, level. Perhaps there is never any history without the installation of a game. Events have to mesh in causal chains, bouncing off given limits, to be something more than the subject of mere chronicles.*

HISTORY is history, but there may be a history to its passing, to its transformation into another form. Here again (with amendments) Georg Lukács: "[The military entertainment complex] destroyed both the spatio-temporal boundaries between different lands and territories and also the legal partitions between the estates. In its [topology] there is a formal equality for all [gamers]; the economic relations which directly determined the metabolic exchange between men and nature progressively disappear. Man becomes, in the true sense, a [gamer] being. [Gamespace] becomes the reality for man. Thus the recognition that [gamespace] is reality becomes possible only under [the military entertainment complex], in [topology]. But the [military entertainment complex] which carried out this revolution did so without consciousness of its own function; the [agonistic] forces it unleashed, the very forces that carried it to supremacy seemed to be opposed to it like a second nature, but a more soulless, impenetrable nature than [topography] ever was."* *SimEarth* prompts a surprising theoretical conclusion: History is back with a vengeance, and where least expected, the historicization of nature. History *on* earth becomes history *of* earth. History becomes total history.

[223]   THE FINAL question for a gamer theory might be to move beyond the phenomena of gaming as experienced by the gamer to conceive of gaming from the point of view of the game. K-Punk: "What do we look like from [game]space? What do we look like *to* [game]space? Surely we resemble a Beckettian assemblage of abstracted functions more than we do a holistic organism connected to a great chain of being. As games players, we are merely a set of directional impulses (up, down, left, right); as mobile phone users, we take instructions from recorded, far distant voices; as users of SMS or IM, we exchange a minimalized language often communicating little beyond the fact of communication itself (txts for nothing?)."* Gamespace is an end in itself.

[224]   THE GAMER might still be tempted to try to leave The Cave, to substitute for its artificial sun an order held in place by

one that really burns in a visible sky. But there is the paradox: you only know the value of that sun, its energy, the consequences of turning it into this or that allocation or resources, because there is a game which at one and the same time depends on its energy yet usurps its place. Only by going further and further into gamespace might one come out the other side of it. Deleuze and Guattari: "One can never go far enough in the direction of [topology]: you haven't seen anything yet—an irreversible process. And when we consider what there is of a profoundly artificial nature . . . we cry out, 'More perversion! More artifice!'—to a point where the earth becomes so artificial that the movement of [topology] creates of necessity and by itself a new earth."* The method for so doing may now be apparent: pressing against the limits of the game from within, to find the other terms forgotten behind the agon. Other terms that may open toward a schizoid complexity or a paranoid complex. Our Virgil, our guide through the overworld of gamespace might in a schizoid light be Gilles Deleuze; in more paranoid shades, Guy Debord: "No vital eras were ever engendered by a theory; they began with a game, or a conflict, or a journey."* And perhaps now by a conflict within and against the game, and a journey through it to get beyond it.

PERHAPS LESS a conflict and more a trifling, a styling, a [225] playing. Mihai Spariosu: "Play is ultimately 'unthinkable'. . . This utopian, or rather atopian, quality of play as the Other of Western metaphysics cannot be approached with critical or analytic tools." Yet after play might arise a mode of being that can be thought—and a gamer theory.

Gamer theory is not about asserting the absolute unique-
ness of games, nor about assimilating them to other forms
(novel, cinema), but rather about marking the game's difference from these forms as something that speaks to
changes in the overall structure of social and technical relations. The form of the digital game is an allegory for the
form of being. Games are our contemporaries, the form in
which the present can be felt and, in being felt, thought
through. From this vantage point, the whole of cultural
history can be rethought. It is not a question of adding
games as the tail end of a history of forms but of rethink-
ing the whole of cultural history after the digital game.
Play may be unthinkable, but it nevertheless has a history,
and that history traverses both cultural forms and the historical form of being itself. To approach it, to think this unthinkable category of play, is to play in and against language. Gamer theory calls for concepts that make the now
rather familiar world of the digital game strange again.

# Cuts

**(Endnotes)**

## AGONY (on *The Cave*)

Steve: "Ahh . . . but I remember the 'cave' when arcades [002] first came out. In my case it was called *Dark Star*. It sucked up a lot of token/quarters. It was totally isolated inside but for the sounds of video games, and black lights with dim tungsten lighting. As I remember it took me entirely out of the external world. It was always a shock to exit dark star and 'reenter' the real world." Julian Dibbell: "The cave, both as abstract figure and as geographical phenomenon, has some other very specific historical resonances in gamespace, via the origins of *Adventure*, the Ur-text of online role-playing gaming."

All unsourced comments are from the *GAM3R 7H30RY* website, where version 1.1 of this text was made available for comment and discussion in a specially designed interface, created in collaboration with The Institute for the Future of the Book. Footnotes usually function to refer back to texts that are prior links in the network of thought to the present work. In the case of these notes from the *GAM3R 7H30RY* website, one can think of them also as a link that refers forward to new networks of thought that have already begun to sprout, however tenuously, from the text, toward the future. See futureofthebook.org.

〖003〗 Sal: "I'm not sure about this assumption that gamers generally don't look at/participate in the 'real world.' It seems to perpetuate the stereotype of the adolescent boy gamer, isolated from the real world, living out a fantasy etc, when actually most gamers are older and don't fit this kind of stereotype at all. I know you are drawing on Plato and trying to pull out a particular point, but I can't help but feel tired of having the stereotype hauled out and given another airing—whatever the point you're trying to make."

Mr Tops: "It's difficult to believe in a person who lives 'entirely' in the cave (although I think I see where you're coming from with the cave metaphor, 'do deformed rabbit, it's my favorite'). My personal perspective on playing PC games is that bright is good. Bright games (like *Halo*) seem more real than dark, dismal games (like *Quake 2*)."

Andrew Jones: "'It's difficult to believe in a person who lives 'entirely' in the cave.' I live in Taipei. I don't speak

Chinese, I don't speak Taiwanese (I am learning though). Everyday after work I play *Counter Strike* for one hour (most days 2) and then maybe play around in *Second Life* for an hour or two. First, in Asia I've seen entire families and individuals that live in computer bars. You commonly find people sleeping in them while their game is still running. In Korea, where many families have small apartments attached to their businesses, some families literally do live in PC bars and sit around farming for each other in *World of Warcraft*. But this is beside the point because these people's circumstances are different than the assumed life the character in these pages has beyond the cave . . . 002 is interesting because the character for a second thinks the real world is less exciting than the game world in the cave. But is this point really that far from reality? People spend hours mining gold in [games like *World of Warcraft*]. These games successfully simulate an environment that appeals to us more than the reality surrounding us. They provide instant feedback for your work. After all when you're at your 'real work' you're not usually aware of how many points, successes, of money you're cracking up per hour/ per minute/ per player etc. . . . What surprises me about the boy who returns to the Cave is his reason. He returns because 'the light' makes everything look 'unreal.' It seems more like the pointless futility of a strip mall would be reason enough to return to something that actually provides you with a reward for a decent day's work (and provides that reward in small lump sums of encouragement every 5–10 seconds no less). Further rambling:

maybe what we need is pay per minute with a little tie in to productivity to make work in real life a little more exciting."

Nick Krebs: "One thing to consider about the transition between the Cave and reality is that the literal space is a bit different than the way Plato considers it. Functionally one is in 'real space' while playing a game in the Cave. One doesn't walk out of the gamespace into the light, one stays put and turns their head or stands up from the computer. Implicit in your argument about the gamer being blinded by the banal reality of the strip mall existence is that reality has been homogenized and is uninteresting compared to the game. I think instead that the transition might be difficult because the space of the game is potentially banal and uncreative, such as dank basements and arcades . . . Also I don't know what job you work for, but the day that my productivity is measured by the minute is the day I end my life. Agon is fun and all, but exploration is also key and doesn't lend itself to a by the minute system."

Andrew Jones: "Actually my point is that a wander around a strip mall doesn't provide as clear-cut rewards as playing a game. I also wasn't referring to sight, but desire. I didn't claim the strip mall blinded the player; the text in 002 did. When you get down to it, what draws people to games is more than visuals or the fantasy environment within, but the way games both play with emotions and create desire and the need to accomplish set goals."

Nick Krebs: "I'm interested to see if this particular distinc- [004] tion between the immense game world and real world will hold. Specifically what about the digital-image environment is alluring and immediately evident and comfortable to the gamer? I'm uncertain what about the real environment is blinding beyond a literal readjustment of the eyes to the sun. And even if the claim is true, that one is blinded by a different kind of knowledge or social organization, doesn't that enhance the immenseness of the real world? A world that one has a partial handle on and can sense that there is much beyond. The reference to the map is also interesting. Assuming we are talking about a gamer who lived in the real world, entered the cave, and has now exited it, the blinding nature of the real could partially be due to having to remap the geography around him/her. Unlike many games, the neighborhood cartography isn't static and is prone to daily change. In *Grand Theft Auto* one usually doesn't find the hospital, gun shop, etc. by wandering the streets looking for visual signature of that type of building, but instead first refers to the map and finds the appropriate symbol and then follows a guided dot to the location . . . Of course there is also convergence of these two worlds, where the real world assumes a homogonous nature from modernization and suburbanization and when *Mapquest* is used to distinguish places rather than architecture."

Lo-rez: "Perhaps you are missing the point. Games are a simplification of life. They have clear set rules, and clear set answers. They give an uncertain person a way to answer certainly and correctly. It provides certainty versus uncertainty. Just try and think of what would happen if a role-playing game had you actually type out your response, instead of picking a canned response. Or a first person shooter that didn't tell you how much health or ammo you had . . . The game itself becomes incredibly complex. If *Grand Theft Auto* didn't have a map, would it be fun?"

[005] Plato, *The Republic,* trans. Desmond Lee (London: Penguin, 2003), p. 243 [516d]. Actually, the translation used here is by Ted Sadler and is quoted in Martin Heidegger, *The Essence of Truth* (London: Continuum, 2002), p. 31. In *Homo Ludens* (Boston: Beacon Press, 1950), Johan Huizinga perhaps first makes this move, of seeing reflective thought and competitive play as not being at odds but rather the former being a consequence of the latter. See also Mihai Spariosu, *God of Many Names: Play, Poetry and Power in Hellenic Thought from Homer to Aristotle* (Durham: Duke University Press, 1991). However, my interest is less in the slippery category of play than in the more formally definable properties of the game. As Gregory Bateson says: "The difference between a game and just playing is that a game has rules." *Steps to an Ecology of Mind* (Chicago: University of Chicago Press, 2000).

Anthony Vidler: "Of course game theory is deeply embedded in all utopias: in the *Republic* Socrates admits that he is playing in words a game normally called 'polis' or 'city,' a board game of strategy between cities once played by Ajax and Achilles, and by Penelope's suitors while waiting for Odysseus' return. More and Erasmus were playing elaborate word games with each other between *In Praise of Folly* and *Utopia*. And Debord's own Kriegspiel seems to have emerged as a formalization of the dérive."

Stephen Wright: "There is an interesting passage in Plato's *Meno,* where Socrates makes use of a makeshift screen—that is, drawing or inscribing (graphein as it were), tracing and erasing figures in the sand—in the course of rediscovering in the inscription the trace of a forgotten truth, creating some sort of rudimentary gamespace. It just may be that this allegory from *Meno* is more closely linked to the Platonic conception of 'gamespace' than the overplayed caves space example."

Twel: "One question about narrative structure: when the [006] gamer emerges from the cave, the 'real' world appears confusing and unrecognizable so s/he returns to the game. Once s/he returns to the 'real' world and is forced to look around, it appears like a game. My question is essentially a 'which came first?' First, did the game precede the real world, structuring the gamer's perception of it? Second, if the 'real' world is as spectral as The Cave, wouldn't the two be equivalent, see Adorno, Debord, Baudrillard; and if so, wouldn't the gamer more easily transition into the 'real'? Also, there is one tension I feel about using the Plato. I think it is really astute comparison, especially with caves being so prominent in the history of gaming. However, for Plato the outside world is the world of the Forms, itself inaccessible by everyday experience. So if we retain the Platonic, as the gamer emerges from The Cave into the 'real' world we are still at one remove from the Forms. In other words, we may be out of the electronic Cave, but we are still within the Platonic cave. From this perspective, it would seem that gaming has prepared the gamer to recognize the spectral existence of the 'real,' or has made him the philosopher. The difference is that there is not, at this point, any indication that there will be another Real behind the society of spectacle."

Jeff Lyons: "Okay. You are making a comparison with Plato's allegory of the cave. Ontologically, you are saying there is a game world and there is a 'real world.' Then you shift and say that 'These games are no joke. When the screen flashes the legend game over, you are either dead, or defeated, or at best out of quarters.' . . . Are you saying that fantasy has overtaken reality, and that the ontological distinction between the fantasy world of video games and the real world (outside the cave) has been blurred?"

[007] Paula Berinstein: "Sorry to be so picky, but 'opiate' isn't a verb."

Kathy Fitch: "I'm not usually a fan of rampant verbing of nouns, either, but there's something kind of fetching about 'opiate' as a verb in this context, because it made me think of Opie of Mayberry, USA—one of the epicenters of imaginary solutions to real problems [on the *Andy Griffith Show*, where Ron Howard played Opie]. So, the poet trumps the grammarian, this time."

Sam Brenton and Reuben Cohen, *Shooting People: Adventures in Reality TV* (London: Verso, 2003), p. 57. See also Mark Andrejevic, *Reality TV: The Work of Being Watched* (Lanham NC: Rowman & Littlefield, 2004).

Lucy Cade: "Interesting how in many games (multiplayer [008] online ones in particular) we recreate real world inequalities. There are top ranks in the game world, ways of knowing that 'we' are better than 'them,' people strive to obtain armor or money (or anything else that = status or power) leading some people to complain that their game has become like a job. Why are some people so conditioned by materialism that they extend it to virtual goods that only exist in a game environment and would be worth nothing if you stopped caring about (playing) that game?"

Slavoj Žižek, *The Fragile Absolute* (London: Verso, 2000), [010] p. 77. I have sworn off the strong brew of a psychoanalytic reading of gamespace here, even using the Žižek (Miller Lite) version, but for intimations of such a reading, see Andrejevic, as noted above.

Notorious B.I.G., "Things Done Changed," from *Ready To* [011] *Die (Remastered)* (Bad Boy Records, 2004). Hip-hop vividly expresses the subjectivity of the player in the zero-sum game of survival. The bodies of black men become the sacrificial sites of the consequences of gamespace. See Eithne Quinn, *Nuthin' But A 'G' Thang: The Culture and Commerce of Gangsta Rap* (New York: Columbia University Press, 2005).

Ed: "'Work is my play 'cause I'm playing when I work,' Beastie Boys, 'Time to Get Ill.' Being a rock star or rap star is a fantasy of the ultimate reconciliation of play and work."

[012] Bob Stein: "Mightn't it be more accurate to say that the people are not interested in playing 'the citizen' when the effort fails to produce a measurable or recognizable effect? However in games like *World of Warcraft*, which value co-operation within guilds or tribes, it seems that gamers are willing to play the role of contributing group member (citizen) . . . I'm not suggesting that one can be a real-world citizen within a game, but that game play can also function in the realm of desire—i.e. that gameplay in some ways, in some cases, seems to function as a substitute for what is lacking in the real-world—in this case, the yearning to be a contributing member of a group, i.e. a citizen."

[013] Roger Caillois, *Man, Play and Games* (Urbana: University of Illinois Press, 2001), p. 114. This text is a standard in game studies, new and old, but rarely is Caillois put back into the political context of his time. In his *Discourse on Colonialism* (New York: Monthly Review Press, 1972), p. 73, Aimé Césaire indicts Caillois as a "thinker who, while claiming to be dedicated to rigorous logic, sacrifices so

willingly to prejudice and wallows voluptuously in clichés." Caillois' version of ethnography is for Césaire premised on the superiority of the West, and while it is a quite different text that Césaire is attacking here, his indictment may also apply to *Man, Play and Games,* which makes a case for the superiority of a certain order of games that is distinctly European.

Paolo Virno, "The Ambivalence of Disenchantment," in [014] Michael Hardt and Paolo Virno, eds., *Radical Thought in Italy* (Minneapolis: University of Minnesota Press, 1996), pp. 17–18. See also the special issue on Paolo Virno, *Grey Room* 21 (Fall 2005).

Raoul Vaneigem, *The Revolution of Everyday Life* (London: [015] Rebel Press, 2001), p. 264. "Subversion" here translates "détournement." Elsewhere Vaneigem writes: "If cybernetics was taken from its masters, it might be able to free human groups from labor and from social alienation. This was precisely the project of Charles Fourier in an age when utopia was still possible" (p. 84).

Guy Debord, *Society of the Spectacle and Other Films* (London: Rebel Press, 1992). Debord was also, later in life, the creator of the *Game of War.* See *Le Jeu de la Guerre: Relevé des Positions Successives de Toutes les Forces au Cours d'une Partie* (Paris: Gallimard, 2006).

Richard Neville, *Play Power: Exploring the International Underground* (New York: Random House, 1970), p. 278. The [016] beautiful freaks, heading toward the suburbs and real jobs, left behind the New Games Movement. See Bernard DeKoven, *The Well-Played Game: A Player's Philosophy* (New York: Anchor Press, 1978).

[021] Karl Marx, "Critique of the Gotha Programme," *The First International and After: Political Writings,* Vol. 3 (Harmondsworth: Penguin, 1974), p. 347. The phrase may have originated with Louis Blanc. In *Rationalizing Capitalist Democracy: The Cold War Origins of Rational Choice Liberalism* (Chicago: University of Chicago Press, 2003), S. M. Amadae points out that "decision technologies" such as game theory were directly the product of attempts to provide an intellectual counter-weight to Marxist theory during the cold war. Where Schumpeter, Friedrich von Hayek, and Karl Popper had all made defenses of liberal capitalism that recognized the intellectual glamor of Marxism, the economist Kenneth Arrow produced a complete and systematic rejection of socialist theory of any kind. In Arrow's hands, this becomes an attack on the very principle of a general will, or the social construction of needs. Arrow, in short, becomes the ideologue of gamespace. Collective rationality, or the rationality of ends, is impossible. Only individuals and their rankings of preferences remain. We return to the consequences of this achievement in "Conclusions." Interestingly, the decision technologies of cold war America find their complete antithesis not so much in Soviet social planning as Situationist critique. Where rational choice theories attempt a concept of game that excludes play, the Situationists attempt a concept of

play outside the game: from each according to their abilities; to each according to their desires.

Jodi Dean: "I'm intrigued by the reversals—the ones that [022] involve cave, reality, and play. It's quite bold to begin a critique of 'reality'/gamespace from something like a game. On the one hand, it's traditional—like any allegory. On the other hand, folks like to think that we somehow judge the game against reality or illusions against something we think of as true. What a bizarre neo-post-retro Platonism! So, play becomes the rules within the game and regular old reality is held up against this. I think that game theorists would likely be delighted. I wonder, though, about the loss/erasure of desire. It makes sense that games/gamespace are in the realm of drives—it's not really about the end, it's about getting there—but you really go back and forth between these logics. So, here, it seems that desire would reappear, despite claims to the contrary. And, then I start thinking about good old *jouissance*. Fragmentation seems a little too predictable, planned. But there are disruptions. Games crash. And surely the military entertainment complex crashes a lot. Crassly put—they really fuck up a lot on their own terms. And, what about the ways that the users reconfigure the systems, the games, the technology, going against what's set for them. I'm not convinced that this is usefully re-appropriated into yet another level of game play."

Virginia Kuhn: "I am currently reading Adam Greenfield's [023] *Everyware: The Dawning Age of Ubiquitous Computing*

(Berkeley: Peachpit Press, 2006), and I find its argument about the relationship of the user to the developer of computing systems really relevant here. Greenfield posits the notion that certain ubiquitous systems are engaged inadvertently (load sensors in floors, GPS locators, and of course video surveillance) such that the user makes no conscious decision to interact. Given that in the early days of computing, users were often developers as well, the field was more level. With the growth of a digital world, one simply can't assume a level of proficiency and this changes the stakes considerably. The risks of gamespace, at once violent and harmless, and the insinuation of gamespace into reality and vice versa are the really compelling aspects of this work for me. I think the gap between the roles of theorist and practitioner does need to close in order to ensure a reflective development of games, computing, life."

McKenzie Wark: "Very interesting. It is as if the whole world was now 'object oriented'—programmable in such a way that each process is a black box to the next one, just taking inputs and delivering outputs."

Lars Svendsen, *A Philosophy of Boredom* (London: Reaktion Books, 2005), p. 38. In popular demonology, computer games are supposedly "violent" and a cause of "real" "violence." Oddly, the rise of the computer game in the United States correlates with a significant *fall* in violent crime. If there is a prima facie case to answer, then, it is that computer games *prevent* violence.

Hugh: "I think the single player/multi-player distinction [025] which comes up here is really important. Playing a single player game, I know that what happens doesn't matter, in the sense that it is between me and a computer which I can restart if I don't like how that game's going. Life is a lot more like a multi-player game, but once one acknowledges this, I feel like maybe anthropology sneaks into gamer theory, and games become one social context among others."

Christian McCrea: "I agree that single player games are where the bulk of analytical potential still lies, especially since *World of Warcraft* dominates the online gaming sphere, and with it anthropology dominates its analysis."

ALLEGORY (on *The Sims*)

"SimSmarts: An Interview with Will Wright," in Brenda [028] Laurel, *Design Research: Methods and Perspective* (Cambridge: MIT Press, 2003).

Gonzalo Frasca, "The Sims: Grandmothers Are Cooler Than Trolls," *Game Studies* 1:1 (July 2001), gamestudies.org. Both *Game Studies* and Frasca's own website ludology.org have been extraordinarily useful in the writing of this book.

Fredric Jameson, *Postmodernism, or, The Cultural Logic of Late Capitalism* (London: Verso, 1991), p. 17. The "postmodern" might, in the light of the concept of gamespace and the rise of the computer game as form, appear as a temporary phenomenon. The free-floating signs of the postmodern become the raw material for games which do not restore their meaning or necessity but create for them new quantitative relations of value.

[029]  Walter Benjamin, *The Origins of German Tragic Drama* (London: Verso, 1998), p. 175. The other classic Benjamin text that need be mentioned here is "The Work of Art in the Age of Mechanical Reproduction." The reproduction of the image strips it of its aura by severing the image from the object. As an object, a work of art can be a piece of property. Once the image can be detached from the particular object and its provenance, a kind of "communism of the image" arrives. But once this reproducibility of the image becomes an everyday phenomena, the very foundations of the culture industry are threatened. The game does not restore the aura of the unique work of art as object, but it does introduce a new kind of scarcity, and hence allows the re-establishing of property in the realm of the image.

Walter Benjamin, "Central Park," in *Selected Writings,* Vol. 4 (Cambridge: Harvard University Press, 2003), p. 173. The reproducibility of images not only allows them to escape from property but also from propriety, from rules governing their circulation and the policing of their meaning. This decay of meaning then becomes an allegory for the decay of the whole society which gave rise to it. Here games again perform the work of restoration, but not by restoring meaning so much as assigning numerical value to otherwise devalued signs.

Lev Manovich, *The Language of New Media* (Cambridge: [030] MIT Press, 2001), p. 222. Manovich makes the necessary first step toward a formal theory of games as algorithmic. The algorithm does the work of assigning value to signs. The second step would be a critical theory, based on those formal discoveries, but using them to discover the gap between the form and the world which it is not.

Alex Galloway, *Gaming: Essays on Algorithmic Culture* (Minneapolis: University of Minnesota Press), 2006. Many thanks to Alex for allowing me to see this book in manuscript.

Greg Costikyan, "Algorithmic and Instantial Games," in [031] Amy Scholder and Eric Zimmerman, eds., *Re:Play: Game Design + Game Culture* (New York: Peter Lang, 2003), p. 26. See also Costikyan's consistently interesting blog, costik.com.

Jay David Bolter and Richard Grusin, *Remediation: Under-* [032] *standing New Media* (Cambridge: MIT Press, 1999), p. 45. Bolter and Grusin challenge the cyberhype that insists on the breathtaking novelty of each new iteration of digital media, which they see as an inheritance from modernism. "As we have shown, what is . . . new is the particular way in which each innovation rearranges and reconstitutes the meaning of earlier elements . . . The true novelty would be a new medium that did not refer for its meaning to other media at all" (pp. 270–271). But were that the case, this hypothetical new medium would not be "new"—it would be incomparable. What matters is the qualitative difference in the way the old is both recuperated and transformed in the new form, most recently via the algorithm.

[034] Walter Benjamin, "Central Park," *Selected Writings,* Vol. 4 (Cambridge: Harvard University Press, 2003), p. 186. In gamespace there may be no idler, but there may be what Bernard Suits calls the trifler, who plays the game according to its rules, but not aiming for its prizes. The possibility for critical thought is now internal to the game, to its rules, to its spaces, its conventions, but not to its goals. Which might be the contemporary equivalent of the ancient advice to the theorist to pay one's respect to the local gods, even though one does not believe in them.

[036] Alana Perlin: "I wonder how Sherry Turkle's notion of 'evocative objects' would relate to the idea of assigning meaning to gaming images. If computer characters and imagery are to become more than our facile, attenuated subjects, it seems that we must assign them greater evocative significance." See Sherry Turkle, *Life on the Screen* (New York: Simon & Schuster, 1997).

[040] Bernard Suits, *The Grasshopper: Games, Life and Utopia* (Toronto: University of Toronto Press, 1980), p. 47. This is not just a classic work but a work of art in its own right. It takes the form of a dialogue among the ants about the teachings of the recently departed grasshopper. As per the ancient parable, the grasshopper refused to store up grain for the winter—refused work in the name of play—and died. The ants are left to reconstruct the teachings of the grasshopper. In gamespace, however, we are all grasshop-

pers. The consequences of this relation to time I leave to the concluding chapter.

Steven Poole, *Trigger Happy* (New York: Arcade, 2000), p. 33. This was the first really good attempt at an aesthetic of the game experience, from the point of view of the gamer.

EA Spouse, "EA: The Human Story," November 10, 2004, [043] livejournal.com/users/ea_spouse/274.html.

Blaine Harden, "The Dirt in the New Machine," *New York* [045] *Times Magazine,* August 12, 2001, pp. 34–39.

Koen Vlassenroot and Hans Romkema, "The Emergence of a New Order? Resources and War in Eastern Congo," October 28, 2002, jha.ac.

"Our Philosophy," kemet.com. [047]

"Motorola Position on Illegally Mined Coltan," August 25, 2003, motorola.com/EHS/environment/faqs/.

Kristi Essick, "Guns, Money and Cellphones," *The Industry Standard,* June 11, 2001.

Walter Benjamin, "On the Concept of History," *Selected* [048] *Writings,* Vol. 4 (Cambridge: Harvard University Press, 2003), p. 392. Perhaps now this should read: There is no technology of barbarism which is not also a technology of culture. Such is the military entertainment complex.

[050] EA Spouse, "Frequently Asked Questions," November 1, 2004, livejournal.com/users/ea_spouse/274.html.

Dale Cunningham, "The Sims Busten Out," June 10, 2005, livejournal.com/users/ea_spouse/274.html.

### AMERICA (on *Civilization III*)

[051] Peter Lunenfeld and Mieke Gerritzen, *User: Infotechnodemo* (Cambridge: MIT Press, 2005), p. 57. See also Peter Lunenfeld, *Snap to Grid: A User's Guide to Digital Arts, Media and Cultures* (Cambridge: MIT Press, 2001). But where Lunenfeld wants to do "realtime" theory, it seems to me that being untimely is still one of the great theoretical virtues. Hence *Gamer Theory* concerns itself with a game aesthetic that is already slightly obsolete.

C: "No further back than *Dungeons & Dragons* suggests that *D+D* was not in itself a grand orgy of anarchically collected pasts; its popularity hinged on the very idea of reclamation and re-evaluation of these zones and events that were inhabited by real and fictional pasts smashing together like planes to form a cosmology."

[052] Jacques Derrida, *Dissemination* (Chicago: University of Chicago Press, 1981), p. 69. This connection between topos (place) and topic (meaning) is very clear in Eric Michaels's account of Walpiri culture and adaptation of video to its needs. See Eric Michaels, *Bad Aboriginal Art: Tradition, Media and Technological Horizons* (Minneapolis: University of Minnesota Press), 1994.

James Fenimore Cooper, *Last of the Mohicans* (New York: [053]
Penguin, 1986), p. 20. "Cooper portrays the enormous his-
torical tragedy of those early colonizers, who emigrated
from England in order to preserve their freedom, but who
themselves destroy this freedom by their own deeds in
America." Georg Lukács, *The Historical Novel* (London:
Merlin Press, 1962), p. 65. Lukács then goes on to quote
Maxim Gorky on Cooper's central character, Nathaniel
Bumppo: "As an explorer of the forests and prairies of the
'New World' he blazes new trails in them for people who
later condemn him as a criminal because he has infringed
their mercenary and, to his sense of freedom, unintelligi-
ble laws. All his life he has unconsciously served the great
cause of the geographical expansion of material culture."
In both Lukács and Gorky the erasure of the indigenous
presence indicates the extent to which their own writing is
still part of the same process.

Niall Lucy: "The succession—from the oral to the inscrip-
tive—is too absolute, helping to produce the absolute 'new-
ness' of independent, ahistorical game-space. The presence
of the 'new' here depends, I think, on a false succession."

Adeola Enigbookan: "Let us not forget that telesthesia is [055]
not solely the domain of the police, but is also increasingly
within the purview of (or perhaps is becoming the condition of?) citizenship. See *Google Earth*."

Julian Dibbell, *Play Money, Or, How I Quit My Day Job and* [058]
*Struck It Rich in Virtual Loot Farming* (New York: Basic
Books, forthcoming), ch. 2. Dibbell's book is a brilliant ex-

ploration of the brave new world of massively multiplayer games. I have excluded them from *Gamer Theory*, in part because it is too soon to see far beyond the hype surrounding them. The owl of Minerva flies at dusk: critical thought always appears with something of a lag. One way to avoid being caught up in the latest bout of cyberhype is to look to cultural forms that have already been superseded. This was in part Benjamin's purpose in examining arcades in the era of the department store. Most of the hype about massively multiplayer worlds concerns the extent to which they appear to function as economies that are exactly like the "real world." They thus function to naturalize economic behavior and give it an appearance of inevitability. In this the utopian moment of single player games is lost. The game no longer functions as a more fair, more just version of gamespace, even on its own terms. The game is just as venal and corrupt as gamespace, indeed becomes of a piece with gamespace. This corruption of the atopian game is equivalent to the corruption of the utopian text, as too many lines weave their way into and out of its pages. See Edward Castranova, *Synthetic Worlds: The Business and Culture of Online Gamers* (Chicago: University of Chicago Press, 2005), and T. L. Taylor, *Between Worlds: Exploring Online Game Culture* (Cambridge: MIT Press, 2006).

[060] Georg Lukács, *The Historical Novel* (London: Merlin Press, 1962), p. 43.

[062] Guy Debord, *In Girum Imus Nocte Et Consumimur Igni: A Film* (London: Pelagian Press, nd).

Berthold Brecht, "The Radio as an Apparatus of Commu-    〖063〗
nication," in Neil Strauss, ed., *Radiotext(e)* (New York:
Semiotext(e), 1993), p. 15.

Stephen Wright: "Remember CB radio? What a game that
was! That invisible yet interactive sector of the public
sphere—twenty-three slots on the Hertzian waves—that
had its heyday in the mid seventies, in the wake of the Viet-
nam war, before being rendered obsolescent by the global
technology blitz beginning in the 1980s, that spearheaded
the new post-Fordist economy. This 'Citizens' Band' was a
horizontally organized network, and as such the symbolic
forebear of the Internet forums of today. CB is something
of a case study of how and why such and such technology
'makes it' and some other doesn't. For it is not merely a
technical but also an ideological question as to why the collective banter of CB-space yielded to the individualism of
portable phones. Although the sales pitch always presented CB as a user-friendly informational tool—warning
people about traffic jams and similar hazards of consumer
society—it actually had far less to do with content than
with pure talk; it was always more about networking and
communicating (truckers keeping each other awake at
night) than about the message communicated—though it
had the potential for content. Unlike the cell phones that
replaced it, CB was inherently about group communication: everybody was on the same 23 channels; strictly pri-
vate conversations were not for the airwaves. And unlike
'Ham' radio, the licensing scheme was very open (no test
of Morse code, for instance), so it was open to whoever
could spring for the $200 set at the local radio shack."

[064] Fredric Jameson, *Postmodernism, or, the Cultural Logic of Late Capitalism* (London: Verso, 1991), p. 70. The concept of television as flow comes from Raymond Williams, *Television: Technology and Cultural Form* (London: Routledge Classics, 2003). For an attempt to apply and extend Williams to the computer game, see Stephen Kline, Nick Dyer-Witheford, and Greig De Peuter, *Digital Play: The Interaction of Technology, Culture and Marketing* (Montreal: McGill-Queens University Press, 2003). This book is best read in conjunction with Henry Jenkins, *Fans, Bloggers and Gamers* (New York: New York University Press, 2006). Between them, Kline et al. and Jenkins reproduce the dichotomy between the power of the culture industry versus the agency of its consumers. Henry Jenkins, *Convergence Culture* (New York: New York University Press, 2006), provides some reason to believe that the new "user-created content" approach is breaking down that dichotomy. However, one could see this as just another version of "outsourcing," by which consumers even have to produce their own entertainment, while still paying the culture industry for the privilege. The stand-off between active agents and oppressive industries in cultural studies is the result of certain methodological choices. I try to excavate this in the *Complex* chapter. See also Aphra Kerr, *The Business and Culture of Digital Games* (London: Sage, 2006).

[065] Jean Baudrillard, *Selected Writings* (Cambridge: Polity Press, 1988), p. 212. In one of the few essays on Baudrillard worth reading, Adilkno writes: "In order to

pose the problem of media, we must abandon the classical view of their social function as that of informing the masses. We must prevent our media theory from becoming a lower form of energy of the media themselves. That is why it does not try to ascribe all sorts of (subjective) intentions to the media, but rather allows them their own moment, seduction, or fatal strategy." Adilkno, *Media Archive* (New York: Autonomedia, 1998), p. 202.

Geert Lovink, *Dark Fiber: Tracking Critical Internet Culture* [066] (Cambridge: MIT Press, 2002), p. 338. See also Geert Lovink, *My First Recession: Critical Internet Culture in Transition* (Rotterdam: V2, 2003). These two works chart the rise—and the eclipse—of cyberspace, cyberculture, and cyber studies. The more instrumental, if less critical, version of cyberculture flows out of the collision of the counter culture with the military industrial complex Northern California. On which see: Fred Turner, *From Counter Culture to Cyberculture: Stewart Brand, the Whole Earth Network and the Rise of Digital Utopianism* (Chicago: University of Chicago Press, 2006).

*Sid Meier's Civilization III,* developed by Firaxis Games, [068] published by MacSoft, and designed by Jeff Briggs and Soren Johnson, 2001.

Dominic Pettman: "Sorry to bring this back to level one, [074] but Thomas Pynchon's *Mason & Dixon* (New York: Picador, 2004) is a great example of geo-cultural line drawing, especially in terms of 'America.'"

ANALOG (on *Katamari Damacy*)

[076] S: "Suddenly you (we) are making some great connections—Olympian Games—the great competition: Umm.
Time for coffee. Perhaps time to declare an interest: 45
Years on this planet and I still haven't figured out what the
game *is*. For a while I thought it was 'be clever,' 'worship
god' and 'be nice to people.' Then I realized (too late) it was
'produce wealth and security.' Now I think it is 'find happiness, be creative' but I struggle. Along the way an accident
happened and (with more than a little help!) I brought a
new life, a daughter, now 10 years old, into the game. Un-
planned game strategy and the best thing that ever happened to me. The 'happiness' game isn't working for me
right now. Can I say that? Will you all judge me as a crap
player as a result?"

Anne Carson, *Economy of the Unlost* (Princeton: Princeton
University Press, 1999), p. 13. On the very interesting tem-
poralities of so-called gift economies, see David Graeber,
*Towards an Anthropological Theory of Value* (New York:
Palgrave, 2001). One way to track the transformation of
cultural form through topical, topographic, and topological
times might be to compare Xenophon's *The Persian Expedi-
tion* (Harmondsworth: Penguin, 1972), more commonly
known as the *Anabasis,* with Sol Yurick, *The Warriors* (New
York: Grove Press, 2003), Walter Hill (director), *The Warriors* (Paramount, 2005), and *The Warriors,* developed and
published by Rockstar Games, 2005.

Albert Camus, *The Myth of Sisyphus* (New York: Vintage   [077]
Books, 1991). See *Odyssey* 11.593.

*Katamari Damacy,* designed by Keita Takahashi, developed   [078]
and published by Namco, 2004. The sequel for
PlayStation 2 is *We Love Katamari,* developed by Namco
and published in the United States by Electronic Arts. In
the sequel, the King and the Prince have become so popular from the first game that they have fan clubs. Apart from
this self-referential, "postmodern" element, the game does
not add much to the original that would be of interest here.

Patrick: "'It addresses its subject as a player, as a calculator and competitor.' In *Katamari's* case, Keita originally
wanted to make the game more freeform, without a time
limit restriction, and the play would have been more paidic
and perhaps creative in the choice and pattern of objects
picked up. But then the military entertainment complex
came down and demanded a goal-oriented structure in order for the game to be more marketable."

El Moco: "There is a underlying theme in the game, one of
quiet, hidden terror. Although the game masks the act of
voracious consumption with music and quaint, fluffy images, despair is the final emotion that rises to the top when
those final seconds are reached, when the haunting call of
the sirens sends the prince into a final, frenzied panic to
get *just-one-more-item.* And to begin again? You must always begin again, forever, with no hope, real or imagined,

to satisfy your desire to consume *everything*. When the end is reached, in the final stage, you are offered a chance to perform for the cosmos with no time limit. That brings the endgame gambit to a surreal conclusion, a metaphysical prison with nothing to consume. A wandering prince, condemned to travel the earth for something to pick up, eternally."

[079] Christian McCrea: "Again, the bursting out of the sensation of play from its confines is key. Game culture's myriad associations are exploratory and expansive in a way that doesn't quite cohere with our ideas of participatory culture and emergent discourses à la Henry Jenkins, although he was among the first to identify those patterns; games imprint the eternal catastrophe of the digital environment upon us to take elsewhere."

Jesper Juul, *Half-Real: Video Games between Real Rules and Fictional Worlds* (Cambridge: MIT Press, 2005), p. 201. "To play a video game is therefore to interact with real rules while imagining a fictional world" (p. 1). Or in other words, they combine agon with what Caillois calls mimesis. But what goes unexplained is why these rules should be considered more real than the conventions of fiction.

Brenda Laurel, "Coda: Piercing the Spectacle," in Katie Salen and Eric Zimmerman, eds., *The Game Design Reader: A Rules of Play Anthology* (Cambridge: MIT Press, 2006), p. 868. This essay also offers this striking variation on the theme of the "web": "Commercials and brands, spam and flickering web ads, friendly text messages from your cellular service provider, product placements in movies and computer games, all reminding—or rather un-minding—us of the web of politico-consumerism in which we are enmeshed like spider's snacks, stashed for hungry marketers and politicians. The spectacle holds us fast" (p. 867). Brenda Laurel is the first person I ever heard use the expression "military entertainment complex," at the SIGGRAPH conference in Orlando, Florida in 1991. See also Brenda Laurel, *Utopian Entrepreneur* (Cambridge: MIT Press, 2001), on the difficulties of launching her Purple Moon company, which tried to design games for girls.

[082] Paul Virilio, *Negative Horizon* (London: Continuum, 2005), p. 37. In Virilio is a constant sequence of symptoms, the accounts of which are often brilliant, sometimes nutty, but which never quite point to a consistent theory. Two distinctions clarify things among these shifting Virilian sands. The first is between transport and telesthesia. The bifurcating of movement into two speeds—one for things, another for information that begins with the telegraph—is a key moment upon which Virilio doesn't really dwell. The second is between analog and digital information. The coming together of these two developments—digital telesthesia—is the condition of possibility of topology. It is a possibility latent in the telegraph but not fully realized until the age of the internet.

[087] Julian Stallabrass, "Just Gaming: Allegory and Economy in Computer Games," *New Left Review* 198 (March–April

1993): 96. In this remarkable essay, Stallabrass elaborates a critical theory of games using Walter Benjamin's writings on allegory and Theodor Adorno on the culture industry.

[089] Paul N. Edwards, *The Closed World* (Cambridge: MIT Press, 1996), p. 103. See also Manuel De Landa, *War in the Age of Intelligent Machines* (New York: Zone Books, 1991).

Anthony Wilden, *System and Structure* (London: Tavistock, 1980), p. 168. See also Anthony Wilden, *The Rules Are No Game: The Strategy of Communication* (London: Routledge & Kegan Paul, 1987). Wilden's unjustly neglected work combined American cybernetic theory, derived from Bateson, with a broad knowledge of French theory and a political impulse.

[090] Brian Sutton-Smith, *The Ambiguity of Play* (Cambridge: Harvard University Press, 1997), p. 1. In this stunningly comprehensive work, the veteran play theorist solves the problem of the ambiguity of play by suggesting that play *is* ambiguity. His strategy is to study the distinctive rhetorics by which play is invoked. I have chosen to concentrate on the concept of game rather than play. The game, unlike play, is relatively easy to define. Play is what is excluded from any definition of game to give it the appearance of self-consistency.

[094] Drew Milne, "Aftermaths," in *Go Figure* (Cambridge: Salt Publishing, 2003), p. 102. A text that also contains this warning, about method: "One of the unintended conse-

quences of avant garde ambition is the pervasive pleasure taken in reductive but avowedly radical forms of contextualization, from situationism to cultural studies. Oscillations between purification and transgressive collation fall victim to the abstract identity of purity and impurity" (p. 98).

J. C. Herz, *Joystick Nation* (Boston: Little, Brown & Co.,   [095] 1997), p. 205. For a narrative account of the intertwining of military and entertainment industries which updates Edwards, see Ed Halter, *From Sun Tzu to Xbox* (New York: Thunder's Mouth Press, 2006). Also of interest is the documentary film *World War Virtual* (New York: IFFI Productions, 2006).

Johan Huizinga, *Homo Ludens* (Boston: Beacon Press, 1950),   [097] pp. 74–75. "Only through an ethos that transcends the friend-foe relationship and recognizes a higher goal than gratification of the self, the group or the nation will a political society pass beyond the 'play' of war to true seriousness" (p. 211). (Take that Carl Schmitt!) What seems lacking in much writing on games lately is this sense in Huizinga that there is something, ironically, at stake, that agon between conceptions of the game matters more than the details of any particular game.

Chris Taylor, "The Allure of a Sticky Ball," *Time*, May 23,   [098] 2005, p. 56. Some of the more interesting commentary on Katamari has focused on the question of consumerism. Rylish Moeller: "Katamari is an interesting game to discuss since it calls issues like consumerism and environmentalism to the foreground in a very overt sort of way. My worry is not that games are too complicated or too violent or too masculine or too racist but that they are these things in order to perpetuate consumerism." See futureofthebook.org and the techrhet listserver at interversity.org.

[100]  S: "Well we've parted mindsets in this chapter. I observe (1) I don't think there is that much digital in the minds of US Marines on the streets of Baghdad or in the mind of a suicide bomber in Palestine. (2) I think that here, for the first time, the author (a gamer) has brought a personal focus to the thesis. (3) This chapter requires heavy re-write if the objective is to suggest the military entertainment complex has a 'mind of its own' and convincing everyone of that is unlikely. So . . . where do we go now? Read On . . . "

Virginia Kuhn: "I just don't see the passage suggesting that military entertainment complex knowingly subsumes the digital for its own purposes. The whole point of hegemony is that there are competing forces or sparring agendas, but then a tendency forms and gains momentum—sometimes a mob mentality—but the point is that there is no preset practice (for how could one predict every single contingency) but rather a responsiveness, the ability to shift events' meanings to suit a particular interpretation."

Chris Burke: "I think there is a tendency to see everything the digital does as negative in this section. For example, didn't the digital enable the many-to-many nature of the internet? Isn't digital media more free in a number of ways? Doesn't the digital enable a more democratic flow of information? Yes, that may be about to change, but not due to the nature of the digital, but to some very specific Real World desires of powerful corporations. And the game companies, by the way, are against it."

McKenzie Wark: "I'm speaking to a more fundamental layer: that there's always something lost in the digital. It is based always on a primary break or gap. Yes, we can build lots of wonderful things on that break (starting with language) but the 'thing lost' on the other side of the break will come back to haunt us. On which see the *Complex* and *Conclusion* chapters."

ATOPIA (on *Vice City*)

*Grand Theft Auto: Vice City,* developed by Rockstar Games [101] and published by Take-Two Interactive, 2002. It is part of the long running *Grand Theft Auto* "franchise."

Terry Eagleton, *Figures of Dissent* (London: Verso, 2003), p. 24.

Adam Greenfield: "As above, so below, apparently: one of [102] the most thought-provoking things I've heard said recently is that 'there can be no utopia on a planet with six billion people.' Or maybe we always already live in Liberty City."

Mark Amerika: "'What *is* utopia?' is my question. Not what [103] *was.* I have oftentimes asked myself this question because there are times when I think I'm experiencing it. That is to say, for me it must be something that can be experienced—and not just in some sci-fi sort of way."

Fredric Jameson, *Archaeologies of the Future* (London: Verso, 2005).

William Morris, *News From Nowhere* (London: Penguin, 1993), p. 113. Read together with Edward Bellamy's *Looking Backward* (New York: Random House, 1982), these two utopias provide an unwitting genealogy for a gamespace to come. It's a question of seeing the playful side of Morris's craftspeople together with the technocracy of Bellamy's socialist labor. The former is not necessarily anti-technological, and the latter not necessarily purely rationalist. One of the virtues of the Situationists was to see the possibilities to come from reconciling this opposition—if not the dangers.

[104]  Alexander Bogdanov, *Red Star: The First Bolshevik Utopia* (Bloomington: Indiana University Press, 1984), p. 87. Bogdanov's "tektonics" is a neglected counterpoint to "western Marxism," and forerunner to systems theory.

[105]  Edwin Black, *IBM and the Holocaust* (New York: Three Rivers Press, 2002), p. 73. The Holerith provides the answer to the usually unasked question of exactly how someone like Eichmann got the trains to run on time.

[107]  Russell Jacoby, *Picture Imperfect: Utopian Thought for an Anti-Utopian Age* (New York: Columbia University Press, 2005), p. 13.

Roger Caillois, *Man, Play and Games* (Urbana: University [209] of Illinois Press, 2001).

Michel Foucault, "Other Spaces," at foucault.info. The Foucault of the "disciplinary" apparatus seems to appeal to academics because the disciplinary procedure so accurately describes the experience of higher education. It may, however, have little relevance elsewhere. Foucault's celebrated writings on Bentham's Panopticon overlooks the fact that, rather than build it, the British government favored transportation to the colonies, a kind of power that has nothing to do with the disciplinary and everything to do with the vectoral. A better source on the origins of contemporary forms of power would surely be Bernard Smith's *European Vision and the South Pacific* (New Haven: Yale University Press, 1985). It is but a short line from Captain Cook and the chronometer, accurately mapping the world in both latitude and longitude for the first time, to Secretary of Defense Donald Rumsfeld using global positioning satellites to mount a high-tech aerial assault on Iraq. To put the Panopticon in perspective, see Rem Koolhaas and the Office of Metropolitan Architecture, *S,M,L,XL* (New York: Monacelli Press, 1995),which includes a fascinating project for a Dutch prison that was designed to be "panoptic" but in which the celebrated central guard house was actually being used as a coffee stand for the guards, in full view of the prisoners, thus completely reversing the original intention. For a more interesting Foucault, see the account of his adventures in American gay cultural heterotopias, in James Miller, *The Passion of Michel Foucault*

(Cambridge: Harvard University Press, 2000). This is the Foucault who is still with us, the one who, like the "number" that he was, wrote to have no face, and left it to the police to see that his papers were in order.

[110] David Parry: "I think there are places where this 'rank artifice' crosses over from one heterotopia into another, where it doesn't amount to anything quantifiable, but then again it does amount to a change. I am thinking here that one of the things I find fascinating about *Grand Theft Auto* is the way that players create their own value in the game. Certainly within the rules of the gamespace (i.e. the algorithms) but outside the rules of the 'missions.' A sort of re-negotiation of the gamespace. But this re-negotiation doesn't take place solely within the gamespace either. Often it bleeds over (in fact I think it is only made possible by) discussion boards and a proliferation of text around *Grand Theft Auto*. So players come to debate and rehash the value, what constitutes a 'good playing,' but this is never really finally determinate, there is nothing within the game world to measure this. Not only did I rob the bank, but I did so wearing an outfit from the Gash, wielding only a golf club . . . "

Sam Tobin: "I think this . . . gets at what to me is a difficult and attractive notion to tease out, what is the relation between style and play? Or is the fun we have with and through *Grand Theft Auto: Vice City* affect plus effect in order to create an event or goal in a space which ei-

ther has them or where they are boring (assigned missions)?"

Guy Debord, *The Society of the Spectacle* (New York: Zone    [111]
Books, 1994), s. 191. Key to Debord's understanding of
"spectacle" is the concept of separation. Some argue that
the "interactive" quality of contemporary media can, or at
least might, rescue it from separation and its audience
from passivity. One could with more justice see it the other
way around: whatever has replaced the spectacle impov-
erishes it still further, by requiring of its hapless servants
not only that they watch it at their leisure but that they
spend their leisure actually producing it. Play becomes
work.

Work becomes play: Pat Kane, *The Play Ethic* (London: Pan    [112]
Books, 2004), p. 30. This book is a fascinating guide to the
consulting class, to which Kane belongs, which would
bring play into the workplace, and why, "when you get a
taste of genuinely unalienated labor, then even the slightest alienation comes to seem like a temporary stay in the
prison house" (p. 258). While generally heterotopian sports
have been avoided by theory, Brian Massumi has an in-
triguing discussion of Bruno Latour and Michel Serres on
soccer in *Parables for the Virtual* (Durham: Duke University
Press, 2002).

Ralph Rumney, quoted in Alan Woods, *The Map Is Not
the Territory* (Manchester: Manchester University Press,

2000), p. 62. See also Ralph Rumney, *The Consul* (San Francisco: City Lights Books, 2002).

[116] Alberto Iacovoni, *Game Zone: Playgrounds between Virtual Scenarios and Reality* (Basel: Birkhäuser, 2004), p. 83. See also Francesco Careri, *Walkscapes: Walking as an Aesthetic Practice* (Barcelona: Editorial Gustavo Gil, 2002).

George Perec, *W or the Memory of Childhood* (London: Collins Harvill, 1988), p. 159. See also Harry Matthews, *Oulipo Compendium* (London: Atlas Press, London, 1998).

[125] Stephen Duncombe: "*Vice City* and all the *Grand Theft Autos* both share something in common with, but are also radically different than, utopia. Utopia might mean 'no place' but the problem with the utopias of More and Bellamy and others is that it is all too clearly someplace. It is perfection, the end of history. ('Actually existing socialism,' as Stalin had the audacity to proclaim.) Boring. Static. Dead. What excites me when I play *Grand Theft Auto* is that the 'magic circle' of the gameplay is relatively open. Yes, it is bounded in the end (it is guided by algorithms after all), but it takes a long time to discover those boundaries, and the fun lies not in completing the missions but in the exploration and the mastery of the space. I believe the reason that *GTA* is so popular—besides good ole-fashioned vicarious violence—is because of this relatively open play space. To me this suggests a new way to think about utopia and politics. That is: build space to ex-

plore into the very architecture of utopia itself. Utopia should not be an end point but a playing field.

Chris Burke: "Game designers call this the 'sandbox elements' and they are thought to extend the gameplay past the point where the player gets bored."

Christian McCrea: "Games have become theory's sandbox."

BATTLE (on *Rez*)

*Rez*, developed by United Game Artists and published by SEGA, 2002. As Andrew Chang, aka ArC, writes: "This trigger mechanism works the same way in Sega's *Panzer Dragoon* series, which predate *Rez* and are an obvious influence." [126]

Ben: "Not necessarily true. If you want the special, 'true' Pink Butterfly ending, you must achieve 100% shoot down on Area 5, Fear." [127]

Blaise Pascal, *Pensées* (London: Penguin, 1995), s. 47.

Steven Poole, *Trigger Happy* (New York: Arcade, 2000), p. 169. [130]

Niall Lucy, *A Derrida Dictionary* (Oxford: Blackwell, 2004), p. 44. [135]

Jacques Derrida, *The Gift of Death* (Chicago: University of Chicago Press, 1995), p. 44.

[136] Christian McCrea: "I have recently been going back over *Rez* and over music games to find myself the constant reference to language; the enemies are not pure abstract, but linguistic elements from the cultures represented. Mizuguchi begins his talk of *Rez* with footage of poor women in South Africa in 1991 banging drums to call and response, and he points out carefully that it is the shouting that sets the rhythm, not the drumming, and that synesthesia is more about a break in lucidity that comes only when we have gathered enough language to break down in the first place. If the enemies are made up of pre-linguistic fragments, and your journey through to Eden is by the repeated hacking of these languages—and the *styles* of languages represented by the four cultures. Watch how as you pass the great wall motifs, the enemies appear as script. It's merely a motif, and I agree that they can't be taken seriously, but there's a very thick connection in *Rez* between language and music that remains forceful. You are hacking historiography, after all. World 5 represents the digital-natural, evolving worm-viruses, etc. None of this really touches on targeting which is your concern in this area."

[139] Alex Galloway, *Protocol: How Control Exists after Decentralization* (Cambridge: MIT Press, 2004), p. 30. See also Wendy Hui Kyong Chun, *Control and Freedom: Power and Paranoia in the Age of Fiber Optics* (Cambridge: MIT Press, 2006), p. 5: "The problem is not with the control protocols

that drive the internet . . . but rather with the way these protocols are simultaneously hidden and amplified."

Samuel Weber, *Targets of Opportunity* (New York: Fordham [140] University Press, 2005), p. 105. Weber's starting point is Homer (Odysseus taking aim at Penelope's suitors) and Thucydides. "What Thucydides' *History of the Peloponnesian War* suggests is that the more one makes such targeting the paradigm of all action, the more that which is denied returns as the 'missed opportunity,' which is all that remains of chance when its singularity is shunted aside" (p. 21). The parallel between the targets selected by Athens under its demagogues and the United States under its—and the consequences—need not be labored.

Mark C. Taylor, *Confidence Games: Money and Markets in a* [143] *World without Redemption* (Chicago: University of Chicago Press, 2004), p. 295.

*Rez,* Sega, 2001, manual p. 5.

Wassily Kandinsky, *Concerning the Spiritual in Art* (New [146] York: Dover Press, 1986), p. 25.

Jane Pinckard, *Gamegirl Advance,* October 26, 2003, [147] gamegirladvance.com/archives/2002/10/26/ sex_in_games_rezvibrator.html.

Samuel Weber, *Targets of Opportunity* (New York: Fordham [149] University Press), 2005, p. 21.

James Der Derian, *Virtuous War* (Boulder: Westview, 2001), p. 45.

[150]   Roland Barthes, *Sade, Fourier, Loyola* (Baltimore: Johns Hopkins University Press, 1996), p. 150.

BOREDOM (on *State of Emergency*)

[151]   Theodor Adorno and Max Horkheimer, *Dialectic of Enlightenment* (London: Verso, 1979), p. 88.

[152]   Louis Aragon, *Paris Peasant* (Boston: Exact Change Press, 1994), p. 127. This text is also one of the keys to the Situationist concept of the city as the space of games.

June Edvenson: "re: 'all the same after all' I would say: no: in Europe, where I live we're 'all the same'—in America, one is allowed to be a 'star' or 'rich'—i.e. it's okay. I'd say: 'and because here we are all equal and all stars, after all'— something more on this line. This is how the American, of which I am one, is seen in the world right now."

[153]   Arthur Schopenhauer, 'On the Suffering of the World,' *Essays and Aphorisms* (Harmondsworth: Penguin, 1970), p. 43.

Le_Candide: "I cannot not intervene: only reading Schopenhauer's viewpoint should not comfort us in that life of worry and toil, fearing every freed time as a potential gulf of boredom. Leisure or 'schole' as the Greeks used to say (and which gave 'school') is what you win over your workday, it is one of the few meaningful moments, where you can practice philosophy, science, where you can meditate or share time with your loved ones. Just because United States citizens do not have any spiritual life whatsoever, are depressively materialistic and collapse under their fat, does not mean that the whole world is following their example."

John Berger, *The Shape of a Pocket* (New York: Pantheon, 2001), p. 12. John Berger, the poet of necessity.   [154]

Buzzcocks, "Boredom," *Spiral Scratch EP* (New Hormones, 1976). The affirmation of boredom is the true hallmark of punk.

Cyril Connolly, *The Unquiet Grave* (New York: Persea Books, 1981), p. 84. The reference is to Thomas De Quincey, *Confessions of an English Opium Eater* (London: Penguin, 2003), a cherished text of the Surrealists and Situationists.

Kafkaz: "Who could blame play for dancing forever just beyond the reach of anyone who wanted to use it as a fulcrum for anything other than, say, launching water balloons? The delicious boredom of sultry summer afternoons can lead to play that does open the way to discovery: the upside down bicycle whose blur of spokes speaks of gestalt, illusion, persistence of vision, flicks, an intricate play of concepts flashing and spinning in that moment of spontaneity. But play sulks and wanders off when gamers try to box it up, and mourns those who mistake depression for boredom."

[155] Georges Bataille, *The Accursed Share*, Vol. 1 (New York: Zone Books, 1988), p. 106.

[156] Karl Marx, *Capital*, Vol. 1, Part III, ch. 10, sec. 5.

[157] Martin Heidegger, *The Fundamental Concepts of Metaphysics* (Bloomington: Indiana University Press, 1995), p. 96.

[158] *State of Emergency*. Developed by the Scottish firm VIS Entertainment and published by Rockstar Games, 2001, this is exactly the sort of game you would expect from a generation that grew up on British post punk and the Situationists, even if, from the point of view of the latter, it is the ultimate recuperation. It would be tempting to read *State of Emergency* through Giorgio Agamben's *State of Exception* (Chicago: University of Chicago Press, 2005). However, our interest is in the extent that protocol precedes law. In a "state of emergency" what matters is whether the lines of communication still function. This is entirely prior to the question of whether or not the law is to be suspended, creating a "state of exception." See further Lawrence Lessig, *Code and Other Laws of Cyberspace* (New York: Basic Books, 2000).

Heidegger, *The Fundamental Concepts of Metaphysics*, p. 109.

Iggy Pop, "I'm Bored," now most easily found on *The Best* [159] *of Iggy Pop* (BMG, 2005). A distinctively affirmative, assertive boredom here.

Lars Svendsen, *A Philosophy of Boredom* (London: Reaktion Books, 2005), p. 109. Svendsen's conclusion: "Boredom has to be accepted as an unavoidable fact, as life's own gravity. This is no grand solution, for the problem of boredom has none." To which one must counter-pose the Situationist slogan, that "boredom is always counter-revolutionary." Naturalizing boredom merely lets gamespace off the hook, absolving it of any responsibility for our inability to make our own history, and thus escape boredom.

Gang of Four, "At Home He's a Tourist," *Entertainment!* [161] (Rhino/WEA, 2005). In announcing in 1979 that the new entertainment is guerrilla war struggle, Gang of Four prefigure not only *State of Emergency* but much of the contemporary world. Gang of Four popularized the Situationist technique of accounting for boredom as a political symptom, but they did it in a language of the everyday inherited from British pop lyricists such as The Kinks' Ray Davies, and with their own distinctive tone and rhythmic conception of time.

Heidegger, *The Fundamental Concepts of Metaphysics*, p. 77. [163] Here surely is the voice of that Heidegger who was also a fashion victim, prey for the authoritarian currents of his times.

[164] Karl Marx, "18th Brumaire of Napoleon Bonaparte." And yet paradoxically the gamer may make history precisely by not making it, by refusing gamespace in favor of the game, like the players in Satyajit Ray's *The Chess Players* (Kino Video, 2006).

[166] Giacomo Leopardi, *Zibaldone: A Selection* (New York: Peter Lang, 1992), p. 73. Together with Chamfort, Leopardi is that rare example of the progressive pessimist.

[168] Giorgio Agamben, *The Open: Man and Animal* (Stanford: Stanford University Press, 2004), p. 67. The other Agamben work worth mentioning here is *State of Exception* (Chicago: University of Chicago Press, 2005). Topology admits no state of exception. It is not governed by law but by protocol.

[170] Gilles Deleuze and Felix Guattari, *A Thousand Plateaus* (Minneapolis: University of Minnesota Press, 1987), p. 257.

Giorgio Agamben, *The Open: Man and Animal* (Stanford: Stanford University Press, 2004), p. 70.

[171] Naomi Klein, "Signs of the Times," *The Nation,* October 22, 2001. And, one might add, vice versa.

[172] Alan Liu, *The Laws of Cool* (Chicago: University of Chicago Press, 2004), pp. 77–78. This fascinating book makes "cool," that obscure object of desire, the elusive little object

that drives gamespace. But I prefer to see cool negatively, as a false object, posited as the imaginary yet utterly necessary obverse of the real driving force of gamespace—boredom. Coolness is the free market equivalent of grace, a sign of its God, of maximum utility.

James P. Carse, *Finite & Infinite Games: A Vision of Life as Play and Possibility* (New York: Ballantine, 1986), s. 4. [175] Carse offers not so much a gamer theory as a gamer theology, or perhaps even theodicy. For Carse, there are both finite and infinite games, and evil results from the limiting of the infinite to the finite. Yet the existence of infinite games is to be taken on faith. If a gamer theory is to separate itself from a gamer theology, then the existence of an infinite game, of being, form, or spirit outside The Cave has to be held in suspension while the gamer trifles within the finite game, whose existence is discovered in the act of gaming.

### COMPLEX (on *Deus Ex*)

*Deus Ex: Invisible War,* developed by Ion Storm and published by Eidos Interactive, 2003. Designed by Harvey Smith. [176]

Samuel Tobin: "One thing interesting here, and in this subsection in general, is the robustness of the colonizing logic at play. Games can and have been discussed as flighty and hard to pin down, fragile (Bernard Suits). It seems we can do so much to inhabit the progress of a game just by not suspending disbelief, but like computer-grade speed logics or money, all that's needed is for enough of the right people to believe in the game and then we all have to play right? What (y)our Complex does is reverse the ephemeral quality of not only games but of any interface/engagement. I hear echoes of Paul Virilio's *The Information Bomb* (London: Verso, 2006), and its detonation, a pure war, not of excess death but of zero births. We have to play and we have to keep putting our quarters in to boot."

[179] *Deus Ex,* designed by Warren Spector and Harvey Smith, developed by Ion Storm and published by Eidos Interactive, 2000. The original is overwhelmingly preferred to the sequel by gamers, who consequently have less to say about the sequel. Gamer theory might be drawn to what doesn't quite work rather than what most satisfies the fan.

KGS: "Gah, rewrite the section using the first *Deus Ex* game. Not only was it a much, *much* better game, but the player base was much greater and you're more likely to grab the readers' attention if they are familiar with your subject matter."

Mr Staypuft: "Yes, definitely use *Deus Ex 1* instead. It appears in many 'Top 10 PC Games of all time' lists, whereas the sequel certainly does not."

Alexbb: "Actually, the first game also has three different choices at the end, which are each more compelling than anything offered by the second game. One of the things I didn't like about *Invisible War* is that it sought to make it so all three endings came about, and then rehashes what is basically the exact same story. (I could go on and on about what's wrong with *Invisible War*, from a game design point of view.)"

JohnR: "As someone who has completed the first *Deus Ex* several times but never played the sequel to any meaningful depth, perhaps I am not qualified to comment on what you have written. However, it seems to me after having read it, I question whether you are not reading too much into the symbolism of the game itself. I think the game designers set out to create a thoughtful game with more depth than one might expect from many games; however, it behooves the player (and perhaps the theorist) to keep in mind that the main objective of the designer was to provide a piece of entertainment with broad enough appeal to sell to many potential players. In creating his design, I don't think a reasonable designer will incorporate one more whit of theory than is necessary to maximize appeal. I realize that the gamespace relation to reality is most likely only playing out in a subconscious level (perhaps shared?) with the majority of players, but I still have to question how much such consideration actually enters into it to derive entertainment from playing the game . . . I think all the conspiracy stuff and wheels-within-wheels plotting is vastly entertaining, but I certainly don't give the actual powers-that-be in 'real life' enough credit for the kind of cleverness that these games suggest such governing bodies have or even aspire to."

A. J. Greimas, *On Meaning: Selected Writings in Semiotic Theory* (Minneapolis: University of Minnesota Press, 1987), [181]

p. 48. Following Fredric Jameson, here Greimas is more of a key to plotting the codes of ideology than any trans-historical narrative form.

[182] Johan Huizinga, *Homo Ludens* (Boston: Beacon Press, 1950), p. 50.

Greil Marcus, *Lipstick Traces: A Secret History of the Twentieth Century* (Cambridge: Harvard University Press, 1989), p. 361.

Guy Debord, *Panegyric* (London: Verso, 1998), p. 47.

[187] Ice T, "You Played Yourself," *The Iceberg/Freedom of Speech* (Sire, 1989).

[190] Gilles Deleuze and Felix Guattari, *Anti-Oedipus: Capitalism and Schizophrenia* (Minneapolis: University of Minnesota Press, 1983), p. 7.

[191] N. Katherine Hayles, *How We Became Posthuman* (Chicago: University of Chicago Press, 1999), p. 283.

[195] Sigmund Freud, "A Case of Paranoia Running Counter to the Psychoanalytic Theory of the Disease," *Standard Edition*, ed. James Strachey (London: Hogarth Press, 1953–1974), p. 261. And the delusions of psychoanalysts?

[196] Antonin Artaud, *Watchfiends and Rack Screams: Works from the Late Period* (Boston: Exact Change Press, 1995), p. 68.

This counter-posing of Artaud to Freud is of course from Deleuze and Guattari, *Anti-Oedipus.*

McKenzie Wark, *A Hacker Manifesto* (Cambridge: Harvard [198] University Press, 2004), s. 002.

Chris Burke: "Gamers definitely do hack, although maybe always not in the sense that McKenzie uses the term. Rather than creating some new useful service or application, gamer hacks come more from the 'hmm, what's inside this thing' sort of motivation. To the radical mind, there is the advantage here of unlocking some part of the proprietary corporate culture and making it available to the public. Machinima [cinema made with game engines] is one example, and within that world there are several divisions, most importantly hardware hacking vs. software hacking. Much of the machinima world has been embraced and encouraged by the game companies as a way to extend their brand by creating community. But hardware hacking is something that they are firmly against. I have done a little of both and to be honest, for what I do, hardware hacking is less interesting, only because it allows you to do nearly anything with the game and therefore you are no longer working within *their world.* This goes to the core of what I would like to discuss with McKenzie: the thing I love about 'software hacking' a live online game to make something new is the extent to which one is beholden to play within the rules of the game as it was made, while at the same time exercising the ability to bend those rules and thereby make the mass-produced game do something new and more personal. It's as if you got a Hollywood set to yourself for a day and were able to comment on the text of the film by speaking your own lines from within the film itself. This is made more interesting to me by the fact that online gaming is now so pervasive and lucrative for the big companies. I want to believe that we are part of a movement, trail-blazed by the two-way nature of the internet, to bring some democracy to media. I do not doubt that the corporations can put an end to this, but I believe there has been some recent tendency in the game industry to see this sort of hacking as a good thing." See Burke's machinima TV show *This Spartan Life* at thisspartanlife.com.

## CONCLUSIONS (on *SimEarth*)

[201]   *SimEarth* is manufactured by the Maxis company and distributed by Broderbund. As designer Will Wright has acknowledged, it is based on the work of Jay Forrester, particularly his book *World Dynamics* (Waltham MA: Pegasus Communications, 1973). Forrester had previously worked on Project Whirlwind for the US Navy, perhaps the first computer to work in realtime and use video displays.

A much earlier version of this chapter appeared as "Third Nature," *Cultural Studies* 8:1 (January 1994): 115–132.

[203]   Theodor Adorno, *Minima Moralia* (London: New Left Books, 1974), p. 156. On this utopia without prescription, or minimal prescription, see Russell Jacoby, *Picture Imper-*

*fect: Utopian Thought for an Anti-Utopian Age* (New York: Columbia University Press, 2005).

*An Inconvenient Truth,* 2006, directed by Davis [206] Guggenheim, based on a PowerPoint show from the Apple laptop of Al Gore, formerly "the next President of the United States."

Karl Marx, *A Contribution to the Critique of Political Econ-* [210] *omy,* preface.

Cormac McCarthy, *The Road* (New York: Alfred Knopf, [211] 2006), p. 3. McCarthy makes the dystopian novel almost absolute. Interestingly, what returns after the fall is the nightmare of topical space, unmarked, or marked with now illegible lines, and unredeemed by myth. It is the nightmare of the end of gamespace, erasing the protocols of topology with it. "Epistemology is punctuation," said Gregory Bateson. For McCarthy, punctuation is epistemology. *The Road* is written in a language stripped of commas and colons. Its minimalist sentences present a language stripped down to bare topics, where all that is remembered and perceived about the world are signs of danger and the marks of resources for survival. There is so little left beyond subsistence that even games are forgotten. In a rare, safe moment, a father and son make up card games such as Catbarf to replace the forgotten ones. When father and son enter a particularly hellish place, the wallpaper is identified as by William Morris—a rare detail that seems to lack any survival value for anyone to bother remembering.

It is the detail that allows us to juxtapose *The Road* to the utopian tradition. Utopia, for McCarthy, is even more dangerous than murderous cannibals. The ambition of this novel is nothing less than the ruin of any and every utopian hope. But *The Road* is not so much dystopian as, perversely, a malign utopia. The violence that is usually pushed to the margins in utopias is here everywhere, but is the very condition of possibility for the good. "Where men can't live gods fair no better . . . To be on the road with the last god would be a terrible thing" (p. 145). *The Road* is an inverted passion play. The son is the last god, whom his human father will not forsake. But the father has to die for the son. In *The Road* McCarthy realizes that a world which is an almost fully realized topology, with very point connectable to every other, is the ruin of literature. There is no longer a prose than can endow any particular scene with a transcendent dignity. There is no longer a story that can cleave an authoritative line through a landscape. *The Road* is the novel's revenge on a world that has forsaken it.

[212] A. A. Bogdanov, *Red Star: The First Bolshevik Utopia* (Bloomington: Indiana University Press, 1984), p. 80. Bogdanov points to the difficulty of conceiving of totality from within an agon which focuses all one's attention on an opponent. Interestingly, utopian writing may be able to conceive of a totality because of the way it brackets off and ignores its opponents. The utopian writers Bogdanov and Charles Fourier both predicted global warming. See Charles Fourier, *The Theory of the Four Movements* (Cambridge: Cambridge University Press, 1996), p. 48. "The en-

tire world will then be under cultivation, bringing about a rise of five or six degrees." Of course Fourier thought this a good thing, and did really think that the sea would taste like lemonade (p. 50). But being *systematic* thinkers, these utopian writers did bring themselves to think about the way human social relations create—and transform—their conditions as a totality.

Kim Stanley Robinson, *Green Mars* (New York: Bantam, 1995), p. 560. Robinson is also the author of a cycle of novels about global warming, starting with his *Forty Signs of Rain* (New York: Bantam Books, 2004).

Olaf Stapeldon, *Star Maker* (Middleton CT: Wesleyan University Press, 2004), p. 94. In *Archaeologies of the Future* (London: Verso, 2005), p. 124, Fredric Jameson offers this amazing sentence: "Indeed, we may posit that in an achieved utopia, one become unimaginably real and distinct from us in whatever far future or galactic space, the question of art would already have been answered, and *Star Maker* would have turned out to be the *Divine Comedy* of that realized new world, returning to us as a sacred text or scripture mysteriously catapulted from out of the future into our own fallen present, as though it were indeed the enigmatic writing destined to secure a continuity across the barrier of time and historical transformation." In this fallen world, things are a little different, and one can imagine the luckless angels of *Star Maker* traveling the universe observing and communing with the unhappy remains left behind by players of *Spore*.

[214] Franco Moretti, *Modern Epic* (London: Verso, 1996), p. 6. "Formal" here substitutes for "rhetorical." See also Moretti's remarkable essays on literary gamespace, *Graphs, Maps, Trees: Abstract Models for a Literary Theory* (London: Verso, 2005).

[215] Temporar: "While I am reading those pages about games in games I remind myself of a piece of art written by Stanislaw Lem. In a book called *A Perfect Vacuum* (Evanston: Northwestern University Press, 1999), he is reviewing books that don't exist . . . One review really corresponds and even extends what is written here: *The New Cosmogony* is the acceptance speech of a Nobel prize winner in physics. He describes his remarkable theory about the source of physical laws. The universe is more than ten billion years old. Several generations of stars have come and gone. Billions of years have elapsed since the first civilizations could have arisen, so the question becomes, where are they? Why don't we see their names spelled out with galaxies for pixels? His answer is, they are there, in fact they are everywhere, and the structure of physical law is their handiwork."

[216] E. M. Cioran, *Drawn and Quartered* (New York: Arcade, 1998), p. 134. Cioran's seemingly unrepentant fascism should not pass here without mention. See Marta Petreu, *An Infamous Past* (Chicago: Ivan R. Dee, 2005).

[217] Mark Amerika, *How To Be an Internet Artist* (Boulder: Alt-X, 2001), p. 3. Amerika is also the author of the classic interactive text grammatron.com.

Walter Benjamin, "On the Concept of History," *Selected*   [218]
*Writings,* Vol. 4 (Cambridge: Harvard University Press,
2003), p. 392.

Heiner Müller, "The Luckless Angel," *Germania* (New
York: Semiotext(e) Foreign Agents Series, 1990), p. 99.

Plato, *Phaedrus,* trans. Christopher Rowe (London: Pen-   [219]
guin, 2005), p. 63 [274e]. On *Phaedrus* as the key text initi-
ating a critical media theory, see Darren Tofts and Murray
McKeitch, *Memory Trade: A Pre-History of Cyberculture*
(Melbourne: Fine Arts Publishing, 1998), and Darren Tofts
et al., eds., *Prefiguring Cyberculture: An Intellectual History*
(Cambridge: MIT Press, 2004). "Recipe" here translates
the term Derrida made famous: "pharmakon."

David Parry: "Theuth also becomes Hermes the God of
speed and transmission, back to *tele.*"

Niall Lucy: "The move could be too fast here. Derrida's in-
tervention is against the notion of writing as written-down
speech. For him, writing has to be thought as spacing, dif-
ferencing and deferring to see that speech could never
stand 'behind' it."

Jacques Derrida, *Dissemination* (Chicago: University of
Chicago Press, 1981), p. 82. In *Parables of the Virtual* (Durham: Duke University Press, 2002), Brian Massumi ar-
gues that Derrida starts from static terms and works toward uncovering the hidden transit between them, rather
than trying to think movement itself. With this speculative

translation of "pharmakon" as "recipe" I am trying to restore the thought of movement. A recipe (or an algorithm) may be either a poison or a cure, but either way is still a process, a movement.

[220] Manuel De Landa, *War in The Age of Intelligent Machines* (New York: Zone Books, 1991), p. 4. See also Manuel De Landa, *Intensive Science and Virtual Philosophy* (London: Continuum, 2002). De Landa, like Massumi, attempts to restore movement to thought. A play that does not require the game but rather calls it into being.

[221] Patrick Dugan: "'History can no longer be a storyline about free agency constructing its own . . . ' The term 'storyline' in this context is inconsistent. A storyline in a game is an embedded narrative that is always parallel to agency. If you mean that history has purported to be about human agency constructing its own conditions, then 'story' would suffice as a more general term. If you mean to disassociate history from the idea of a story that is told through agency, that is, you suggest that agency had nothing to do with the process of storytelling that constructed history, then it might be better to make this explicit. 'Story' or 'storytelling process' are appropriate direct objects, 'storyline' is not."

Fredric Jameson, *The Political Unconscious: Storyline as a Socially Symbolic Act* (Ithaca: Cornell University Press, 1981), p. 102. Jameson continues: "But this History can be apprehended only through its effects, and never directly as some reified force. This is indeed the ultimate sense in which History as ground and untranscendable horizon needs no particular theoretical justification: we may be sure that its alienating necessities will not forget us, however much we might prefer to ignore them."

Georg Lukács, *History and Class Consciousness* (London: Merlin, 1983), p. 19. The concept of totality, which one can quibble to death in theory, reasserts itself in practice, now that it leaves such telling evidence of its existence—such as global warming. [222]

K-Punk, "Cartesianism, Continuum, Catatonia: Beckett," *Excarnate Thought,* March 26, 2006), k-punk .abstractdynamics.org/. Here gamespace replaced the now archaic term cyberspace. [223]

Gilles Deleuze and Felix Guattari, *Anti-Oedipus* (London: Athlone Press, 1983), p. 321. [224]

Guy Deleuze and Felix Guattari, Anti-Oedipus (London: Athlone Press, 1983), p. 321.

Mihai Spariosu, *Dionysus Reborn* (Ithaca: Cornell University Press, 1989), p. 3. [225]

# Directory

## (Index)